Dearest Chris

we ~

to welc~   ~e

family

To Be a Father

Richard

Adam

Alu   Lou   Bud ♡

Victoria   Rob x.

Other books by Wendi Momen

A Basic Bahá'í Chronology (with Glenn Cameron)
A Basic Bahá'í Dictionary
Call Me Riḍván
Family Worship
Meditation
To Be a Mother

To Be a Father

compiled by

Wendi Momen

George Ronald • Oxford

GEORGE RONALD, *Publisher*
46 High Street, Kidlington, Oxford OX5 2DN

*A catalogue record for this book is available
from the British Library*

ISBN 0–85398–459–X

Typeset by Alexander Leith
www.nineteenmedia.com

Printed and bound in Great Britain by
Cromwell Press, Trowbridge, Wiltshire

Contents

For my grandfathers
Morris Wirtshafter and Hugh Cunningham Morris

my father
Buddy Worth

my husband
Moojan Momen

and my son and son-in-law
Sedrhat Momen and Ashley Southall

Preface

*Only societies that can enlist the energies of men as partners
in the long parenting process can flourish for any length
of time.*

Jonathan Sacks[1]

It is in recognition of the importance of fathers
to their families, to society and to the world
community that this little book of verses from the
holy scriptures, poets and thinkers is offered.

Acknowledgements

My heartfelt thanks to my friends Peter Hulme, Trevor Finch and J. A. McLean, fathers and poets all, who generously offered poems about their own children and families for this volume.

The publisher would like to thank the following for permission to reprint their copyrighted works.

Blake Friedmann Literary TV & Film Agency, Ltd. for quotations from *The Road Less Travelled* by M. Scott Peck.

E. P. Dutton & Co. Inc for 'Patrick Goes to School' by Alicia Aspinwall.

HarperCollins*Religious* for quotations from Jonathan Sacks, *Celebrating Life*.

Mitchell Kennerley for 'Hertha' by Horace Holley, in *Divinations of Creation*.

Penguin Books for 'For a Child Expected' by Anne
Ridler.

Victor Books for quotations from *How to Really Love
Your Child* by Dr Ross Campbell, and from *Family
Fun and Togetherness* by Wayne Rickerson.

Villard Books for quotations from *From Beginning to
End: The Rituals of Our Lives* by Robert Fulghum.

The publisher has made every effort to trace
copyright owners. Where we have failed we offer
our apologies and undertake to make proper
acknowledgement in reprints.

On the Birth of a Child

Man is, therefore, a noble creation,
as perfect as the scheme allows;
a part of the fabric of the all,
he yet holds a lot higher than of all
living things on earth.

Plotinus

Sikh Prayer for the Conception of a Child

God has laid his protecting hand on my head,
on my brow, on my body.
My spirit too is in his keeping,
safe at his blessed feet.
Merciful Guru, keep and protect me,
banish all fear and distress.
Friend of the faithful, Lord of the humble,
ever my refuge and aid.

Guru Arjan[1]

For a Child Expected

Lovers whose lifted hands are candles in winter,
Whose gentle ways like stream in the easy summer,
Lying together
For secret setting of a child, love what they do,
Thinking they make that candle immortal, those
streams forever flow,
And yet do better than they know.

So the first flutter of a baby felt in the womb
Is little signal and promise of riches to come,
Is taken in it's father's name;
Its life is the body of his love, like his caress,
First delicate and strange, that daily use
Makes clearer and priceless.

Our baby was to be the living sign of our joy,
Restore to each the other's lost infancy;
To a painter's pillaging eye
Poet's coiled hearing, add the heart we might earn
By the help of love; all that our passion would yield
We put to planning our child.

The world flowed in; whatever we liked we took;
For its hair the gold curls of the November oak
We saw on our walk;
Snowberries that make a Milky Way in the wood
For its tender hands; calm screen of the frozen flood
For our care of its childhood.

But the birth of a child is an uncontrollable glory;
Cat's cradle of hopes will hold no living baby,
Long though it lay quietly.
And when our baby stirs and struggles to be born
It compels humility: what we began
is now our own.

For as the sun that shines through glass
So Jesus in His Mother was.
Therefore every human creature,
Since its shares in His nature,
In candle-gold passion or white
Sharp star should show its own way of light,
May no parental dread or dream
Darken our darling's early beam:
May she grow to her right powers
Unperturbed by passion of ours.

Anne Ridler

Children are the hands by which
we take hold of heaven.
Henry Ward Beecher

Amadea

It was gently snowing when you were born,
And we were so calm we even remembered,
Despite the sudden onset of labour,
To bring the music and the CD player.

Your erratic heartbeat caused a stir,
And ensured a lot of attention.
It was a long labour and you had
To be assisted out with a venteuse.

To hold you, wrinkled pink and smooth,
Blood-smeared and white-streaked,
In my arms, while you strained to hear
Mozart, was unutterable bliss.

Trevor R.J. Finch

Hertha

She will grow
Beautiful
Beauty will come to her
Given, like sun and rain;
Will go from her
Freely, like laughter
She will be
Centre, circumference to a great joy
Swiftly passing, repassing
Like water in and from a limpid well.
She is of the new generation, new;
Torch for the flame of passion,
Flame for the torch of love.

She will grow
Beautiful.
No, beauty itself will grow
Like her.

Horace Holley[2]

Aurelia

You landed slap on your back
Like an alien astronaut
Thrown from your escape pod
Purple and white, starry-eyed and taut.

Your long arms, flung wide,
Twitched as you blinked in the light.
You kicked, and your husky voice
Rasped the air with your will to fight.

You were on the breast before
The womb-fluid was washed from your head.
In your first bath you were wrinkled and hairy
But your soft skin flushed pink-red.

Your tongue was constantly tasting the air.
You'd come to a different world.
Your hands fanned like jelly-fishes
And when you slept they were tightly curled.

Trevor R.J. Finch

It is not for the love of children that children
are dear; but for the love of the Soul in
children that children are dear.

Brihad-Aranyaka Upanishad[3]

The Baby

Where did you come from, baby dear?
> Out of the everywhere into the here.

Where did you get your eyes so blue?
> Out of the sky as I came through.

What makes the light in them sparkle and spin?
> Some of the starry spikes left in.

Where did you get that little tear?
> I found it waiting when I got here.

What makes your forehead so smooth and high?
> A soft hand stroked it as I went by.

What makes your cheek like a warm white rose?
> Something better than anyone knows.

Whence that three-cornered smile of bliss?
> Three angels gave me at once a kiss.

Where did you get that pearly ear?
> God spoke, and it came out to hear.

Where did you get those arms and hands?
> Love made itself into hooks and bands.

Feet, whence did you come, you darling things?
> From the same box as the cherubs' wings.

How did they all just come to be you?
> God thought about me, and so I grew.

But how did you come to us, you dear?
> God thought of you, and so I am here.
>> *George Macdonald*

Whoever has no children has no light in his eyes.
> *Iranian Proverb*

God has sent this wondrous gift; conceived by grace
> may his years be long.
Boundless the joy of his mother's heart when the
> child appeared in her womb.
Refrain: Born our son, born to adore, faithful
> disciple of God.
His fate inscribed since time began, now given for
> all to see.
Ten months carried then given by God; all sorrows
> flee as joy descends.
His mother's friends sang songs of praise, songs
> which delight the Master's heart.
The mighty vine has seeded again, for God ensures
> that his truth remains.
The guru has granted my heart's desire; my spirit
> stilled, at one with God.

A father earn's his child's respect, and thus I speak as
        the Guru bids.
No mystery dims these words of mine; this child is
        the gift of the Guru's grace.

Guru Arjan[4]

Our birth is but a sleep and a forgetting;
The soul that rises within us,
        our life's star,
Hath had elsewhere its setting,
And cometh from afar:
not in entire forgetfulness,
And not in utter nakedness,
But trailing clouds of glory do we come
From God, who is our home.

William Wordsworth

O Loving Lord!
    To the mountain-stream Thou hast given its
bubbles that dance and tremble and break in light.
    To the forest depths Thou hast given the fresh
flowerbuds that burst and open and unfold their
tender petals in perfect beauty.
    To me Thou hast given the first baby-kiss of this
little one who presses her tiny lips upon my lips in
love.

George Townshend[5]

A child is a bridge to heaven.

Iranian Proverb

Many of our finest human moments are rather small in scale, but large enough in spirit to last a lifetime. Especially when a child is born.

Robert Fulghum[6]

And when God gives you sweet and lovely children, consecrate yourselves to their instruction and guidance, so that they may become imperishable flowers of the divine rose-garden, nightingales of the ideal paradise, servants of the world of humanity, and the fruit of the tree of your life.

Attributed to 'Abdu'l-Bahá[7]

The Importance of Fathers

You only appreciate your father the day
you become a father yourself.

Iranian Proverb

That the first teacher of the child is the mother
should not be startling, for the primary orientation
of the infant is to its mother. This provision of
nature in no way minimizes the role of the father in
the Bahá'í family. Again, equality of status does not
mean identity of function.

The Universal House of Justice[1]

A girl without a mother is like a mountain with no
paths; a girl without a father is like a mountain with
no streams.

Kurdish Proverb

The father makes gurgling sounds for the newborn
infant, although his wisdom be capable of
measuring the universe.

Rúmí

The duty and good works which a son performs are
as much the father's as though they had been done
by his own hand.

Zoroastrian Scriptures[2]

From grandfather Verus I learned good morals and the government of my temper.

From the reputation and remembrance of my father, modesty and a manly character.

From my mother, piety and beneficence, and abstinence, not only from evil deeds, but even from evil thoughts; and further, simplicity in my way of living, far removed from the habits of the rich.

From my great-grandfather, not to have frequented public schools, and to have had good teachers at home, and to know that on such things a man should spend liberally . . .

In my father I observed mildness of temper, and unchangeable resolution in the things which he had determined after due deliberation; and no vainglory in those things which men call honours; and a love of labour and perseverance; and a readiness to listen to those who had anything to propose for the common weal; and undeviating firmness in giving to every man according to his deserts; and a knowledge derived from experience of the occasions for vigorous action and for remission.

Marcus Aurelius Antonius[3]

Whatever there is belonging to the son, belongs to the father; whatever there is belonging to the father, belongs to the son.

Eighth Khanda

When you have children yourself, you begin
to understand what you owe your parents.
Japanese Proverb

The spiritual father is greater than the physical one,
for the latter bestoweth but this world's life, whereas
the former endoweth his child with life everlasting.
'Abdu'l-Bahá[4]

Fathers as Educators

The father of the righteous shall greatly rejoice: and
he that begetteth a wise [child] shall have joy of
him. Thy father and thy mother shall be glad, and
she that bare thee shall rejoice. My son, give me
thine heart, and let thine eyes observe my ways.

Proverbs 23:24–6

O ye who have peace of soul! Among the divine
Texts as set forth in the Most Holy Book and also
in other Tablets is this: it is incumbent upon the
father and mother to train their children both in
good conduct and the study of books; study, that is,
to the degree required, so that no child, whether girl
or boy, will remain illiterate. Should the father fail
in his duty he must be compelled to discharge his
responsibility, and should he be unable to comply,
let the House of Justice take over the education of
the children; in no case is a child to be left without
an education. This is one of the stringent and
inescapable commandments to neglect which
would draw down the wrathful indignation of
Almighty God.

'Abdu'l-Bahá[1]

A father's duty then is to train his son to choose the
right course of his own free will, not from fear of
another; this marks the difference between a father
and a tyrant in the home.

Terence[2]

Were there no educator, all souls would remain
savage, and were it not for the teacher, the children
would be ignorant creatures.

It is for this reason that, in this new cycle,
education and training are recorded in the Book of
God as obligatory and not voluntary. That is, it is
enjoined upon the father and mother, as a duty, to
strive with all effort to train the daughter and the
son, to nurse them from the breast of knowledge
and to rear them in the bosom of sciences and arts.
Should they neglect this matter, they shall be held
responsible and worthy of reproach in the presence
of the stern Lord.

'Abdu'l-Bahá[3]

There's no advice like father's –
even if you don't take it.
American Proverb

Educating Fathers

Happiness is not found in self-contemplation; it is
perceived only when it is reflected in another.
Dr Johnson

A Child

A child's a plaything for an hour;
    Its pretty tricks we try
For that or for a longer space –
    Then tire, and lay it by,
But I knew one that to itself
    All seasons could control;
That would have mock'd the sense of pain
    Out of a grievèd sibyl.
Thou straggler into loving arms,
    Young climber-up of knees,
When I forget thy thousand ways
    Then life and all shall cease.

Mary Lamb

There was one who, being crossed, spoke to his son
in anger, and saw the child's face change in fear.

Thereafter, praying in penitence, he heard the
Voice of the Spirit speak to him:

'Think not to number this weak one among thy
possessions, nor imagine him to be thy creation.
Thou callest him thy son. Yet within his infant soul
lies hidden that which is deeper than thy knowing.
In heaven his spirit stands now among the angels

of My presence, and here on earth the sword of My
justice protects and avenges him against all, and
especially against thee. Love thou thy son, and love
thyself in him. Teach him My way, and walk in it
thyself that thou mayest be his guide. He is not
thine, but Mine. Therefore, in all thou dost with
him keep Me in remembrance, and fear Me. This is
thy duty. See that thou fulfil it always, and slack not
therein.'

George Townshend[1]

Just as a silver smith
        step by
        step,
                bit by
                bit,
                        moment to
                        moment,
        blows away the impurities
        of molten silver –
        so the wise man, his own.[2]

Dhammapada[2]

Fathering

The best way to help a child . . . is to share
your own spiritual life with him.
Ross Campbell[1]

Deliver my longings and greetings to the consolation
of thine eye . . . and to thy younger son . . . Verily
I love them both even as a compassionate father
loveth his dear children. As to thee, have for them
an abundant love and exert thine utmost in training
them, so that their being may grow through the
milk of the love of God, forasmuch as it is the duty
of parents to perfectly and thoroughly train their
children.

There are also certain sacred duties on children
toward parents, which duties are written in the
Book of God, as belonging to God. The (children's)
prosperity in this world and the Kingdom depends
upon the good pleasure of parents, and without this
they will be in manifest loss.
'Abdu'l-Bahá[2]

It is not guided missiles but guided morals
that is our great need today.
George L. Ford

I think the one lesson I have learned is that
there is no substitute for paying attention.
Diane Sawyer

The greatest benefit which we have to confer on you
is: Guidance to God.

When God chose us to be your parents He
commanded us to offer you this guidance.
Therefore, it is by His will that we give you His
Holy Teaching. We speak to you of Him and of
His prophets, we surround you continually with
thoughts of faith and worship, and we never cease
to pray for you. We cannot compel you to learn the
lessons which we teach; we would not compel you
if we could, for God intends our wills to be free.
You must choose for yourself. Your mother and I
are trying – as best we may – to follow the leading
of that Guidance, and it is our hope and prayer that
you will travel with us. We should be very lonely
if we had to take one step without you. For this
teaching which God has given us to pass on to you
is the most precious thing we have to give you: more
precious far than food, or clothes or schooling, or
even life itself – for this knowledge is ETERNAL life.

George Townshend[3]

The great use of life is to spend it for
something that outlasts it.

William James

Happy is he that is happy in his children.

T. Fuller[4]

Ludlow

(Declaration of the Bab)

Beside me your mind moves past the orange tree
   at dawn
      through to His house in Shiraz.
                Idly I
watch a flock of folk bleat heedlessly
past constellations of dandelions.

Beneath, old castle walls disintegrate
before a tower of high and sandstone holiness.

Between ramblers and ruin winds
a dark band of water that plunges its shining
sheer into a roar of foam and
almost stills my unquiet mind as we stand.
To capture it I take a photograph –
an ageing animal hoping to whet
his tarnished and uncertain soul
on the stone edge of a wide cascade this Holy Day.

We carry our sleeping son up the path
renewed after the flood one hundred years ago,
back from the water's lace of light, back from Shiraz,
bearing to the car dreams the shape of tomorrow.

Peter Hulme

The time and the quality of the time that their
parents devote to them indicate to children the
degree to which they are valued by their parents.

M. Scott Peck[5]

I Know a Secret

I know a secret that the night imparts
        When bedtime ends day's honours and
        disgraces
And masquerades all stormy little hearts
        With such deceptively angelic faces!

You shan't forget your green and golden youth,
        Lying some day so dim and far behind you:
So, mingling simple fancy, simple truth,
        Here are these little fables to remind you.

You won't forget. And in all joy and pain.
        Life offers, dear my urchins, when you're
        older,
How Daddy'd love to carry once again
        You, and all your world, upon his shoulder!

Christopher Morley

A happy childhood is one of the best gifts that
parents have it in their power to bestow.

Mary Cholmondeley

A man once wrote to Rav Kook, Chief Rabbi of
pre-state Israel, saying, 'I loved my son. I gave him
everything. And now he has abandoned our faith.
What shall I do?'

Rav Kook replied, 'You loved your son before.
Now love him even more.'[6]

Thy Lord has decreed you shall not serve any but
Him, and to be good to parents . . .

Qur'án 17:23

Children must be most carefully watched over,
protected and trained; in such consisteth true
parenthood and parental mercy.

'Abdu'l-Bahá[7]

Hear me your father, O children, and do thereafter,
that ye may be safe.

The Book of Sirach 3.1

. . . good fathers are likely to have good sons, and
good training is likely to produce good character.

Aristotle[8]

Fathers Educating Children

The one who teaches is the giver of eyes.
Tamil Proverb

Unto every father hath been enjoined the
instruction of his son and daughter in the art of
reading and writing and in all that hath been laid
down in the Holy Tablet. He that putteth away that
which is commanded unto him, the Trustees are
then to take from him that which is required for
their instruction if he be wealthy and, if not, the
matter devolveth upon the House of Justice. Verily
have We made it a shelter for the poor and needy.
He that bringeth up his son or the son of another,
it is as though he hath brought up a son of Mine;
upon him rest My glory, My loving-kindness, My
mercy, that have compassed the world.
Bahá'u'lláh[1]

*And in another Tablet, these exalted words have been
revealed*: O Muḥammad! The Ancient of Days hath
turned His countenance towards thee, making
mention of thee, and exhorting the people of God
to educate their children. Should a father neglect
this most weighty commandment laid down
in the Kitáb-i-Aqdas by the Pen of the Eternal
King, he shall forfeit rights of fatherhood, and be
accounted guilty before God. Well is it with him
who imprinteth on his heart the admonitions of
the Lord, and steadfastly cleaveth unto them. God,

in truth, enjoineth on His servants what shall assist
and profit them, and enable them to draw nigh unto
Him. He is the Ordainer, the Everlasting.

Bahá'u'lláh[2]

Your father has a certain duty, and if he shall not
fulfil it, he loses the character of a father, of a man
of natural affection, of gentleness.

Epictetus[3]

Teach ye your children so that they may peruse
the divine verses every morn and eve. God hath
prescribed unto every father to educate his children,
both boys and girls, in the sciences and in morals,
and in crafts and professions . . .

Bahá'u'lláh[4]

. . . although the mother is the first educator
of the child, and the most important formative
influence in his development, the father also has
the responsibility of educating his children, and
this responsibility is so weighty that Bahá'u'lláh has
stated that a father who fails to exercise it forfeits his
rights of fatherhood.

The Universal House of Justice[5]

When we seek to discover the best in others, we
somehow bring out the best in ourselves.

William Arthur Ward

Child of my heart, call not me your Father; and this
dear wife of mine that gave you birth, call not her
your mother. Think not the home we make for you
is your True Home. The life that is bestowed on you
through us will soon pass away and perish; but you,
my son, you will not perish.

This life is a steed to bear you to the Kingdom of
Eternity, of which you are born a Prince. The Ruler
of that Kingdom is your Father. His Palace is your
Home. You are heir to a mighty princedom because
you are born His son.

Ride straight and fast to take your heritage. Fear
no danger. Stop not for flood nor foe. Look not to
right nor left. Your Father waits for you.

Ride on. Rest not. Remember you are the son of
a King.

George Townshend[6]

It is better to know some of the questions
than all of the answers.

James Thurber

What is a good man but a bad man's teacher?
What is a bad man but a good man's job?
If you don't understand this, you will get lost,
          however intelligent you are.
It is the great secret.

Tao te Ching[7]

Anecdote for Fathers,

Shewing How the Art of Lying May Be Taught

I have a boy of five years old,
His face is fair and fresh to see;
His limbs are cast in beauty's mould,
And dearly he loves me.

One morn we stroll'd on our dry walk,
Our quiet house all full in view,
And held such intermitted talk
As we are wont to do.

My thoughts on former pleasures fan;
I thought of Kilve's delightful shore,
My pleasant home, when spring began,
A long, long year before.

A day it was when I could bear
To think, and think, and think again;
With so much happiness to spare,
I could not feel a pain.

My boy was by my side, so slim
And graceful in his rustic dress!
And oftentimes I talked to him,
In very idleness.

The young lambs ran a pretty race;
The morning sun shone bright and warm;
'Kilve,' said I, 'was a pleasant place,
'And so is Liswyn farm.

'My little boy, which like you more,'
I said and took him by the arm –
'Our home by Kilve's delightful shore,
'Or here at Liswyn farm?'

'And tell me, had you rather be,'
I said and held him by the arm,
'At Kilve's smooth shore by the green sea,
'Or here at Liswyn farm?'

In careless mood he looked at me,
While still I held him by the arm,
And said, 'At Kilve I'd rather be
'Than here at Liswyn farm.'

'Now, little Edward, say why do;
My little Edward, tell me why;'
'I cannot tell, I do not know.'
'Why this is strange,' said I.

'For, here are woods and green-hills warm;
'There surely must some reason be
'Why you would change sweet Liswyn farm
'For Kilve by the green sea.'

At this, my boy, so fair and slim,
Hung down his head, nor made reply;
And five times did I say to him,
'Why? Edward, tell me why?'

His head he raised – there was in sight,
It caught his eye, he saw it plain –
Upon the house-top, glittering bright,
A broad and gilded vane.

Then did the boy his tongue unlock,
And thus to me he made reply;
'At Kilve there was no weather-cock,
'And that's the reason why.'

Oh dearest, dearest boy! my heart
For better lore would seldom yearn,
Could I but teach the hundredth part
Of what from thee I learn.

William Wordsworth

If you can't be a good example, then you'll
just have to be a horrible warning.
Catherine Aird

The hearts of little children are pure, and therefore,
the Great Spirit may show to them many things
which older people miss.

Black Elk, Oglala Sioux[8]

Patrick Goes to School

'I'm going to school tomorrow, just
   To learn to write and read.
I wish I didn't have to, for
   I do not see the need.'

'Do you want to be', said Dad, 'a deep-
   Dyed ig-no-ra-mus, Pat?'
'Oh, no!' I cried, 'I'd hate to be
   A dreadful thing like *that*!

'And so I thought I'd go to school
   To learn to read and write.
So *not* to be that 'deep-dyed' thing
   Dad spoke about tonight!'

          Alicia Aspinwall

Hear, ye children, the instruction of a father,
   and attend to know understanding.
For I give you good doctrine,
   forsake ye not my law.
For I was my father's son, tender and only [beloved]
   in the sight of my mother.
He taught me also, and said unto me,
    'Let thine heart retain my words: keep my
    commandments, and live.
Get wisdom, get understanding: forget [it] not;
   neither decline from the words of my mouth.

Forsake her not, and she shall preserve thee:
     love her, and she shall keep thee.
Wisdom [is] the principal thing; [therefore]
     get wisdom: and with all thy getting get
     understanding.
Exalt her, and she shall promote thee: she shall bring
     thee to honour, when thou dost embrace her.
She shall give to thine head an ornament of grace:
     a crown of glory shall she deliver to thee.
Hear, O my son, and receive my sayings;
     and the years of thy life shall be many.

Proverbs 4:1–10

My son, keep thy father's commandment,
     and forsake not the law of thy mother:
Bind them continually upon thine heart, [and] tie
     them about thy neck.
When thou goest, it shall lead thee; when thou
     sleepest, it shall keep thee; and [when] thou
     awakest, it shall talk with thee.
For the commandment [is] a lamp; and the law [is]
     light; and reproofs of instruction [are] the
     way of life . . .

Proverbs 6:20–3

Truly, the hearts of the children are very pure. This
is why Christ said, 'Be ye like children.'

Attributed to 'Abdu'l-Bahá[9]

My son, keep my words, and lay up my
      commandments with thee.
Keep my commandments, and live; and my law
      as the apple of thine eye.
Bind them upon thy fingers, write them upon
      the table of thine heart.
Say unto wisdom, Thou [art] my sister; and call
      understanding [thy] kinswoman . . .

Proverbs 7:1-4

By crawling, a child learns to stand.
Proverb from Niger

While the children are yet in their infancy feed
them from the breast of heavenly grace, foster
them in the cradle of all excellence, rear them in
the embrace of bounty. Give them the advantage
of every useful kind of knowledge. Let them share
in every new and rare and wondrous craft and art.
Bring them up to work and strive, and accustom
them to hardship. Teach them to dedicate their
lives to matters of great import, and inspire them to
undertake studies that will benefit mankind.

'Abdu'l-Bahá[10]

Children who get everything they ask
for seldom succeed in life.
Proverb from the Philippines

Nothing can be taught: all the teacher can
do is to show that there are paths.

Anon

By divine education at home we mean the creation
of an atmosphere in which the child can breathe the
spiritual powers of this Age, and in due time, like
unto a rose, may blossom out, unfold, and proclaim
his existence in the garden of God . . . This cannot
be achieved by force or any form of compulsion just
as the child's birth cannot be realized by outside
forces. We never try to pull the flower out of its
stem in winter. The flowers will adorn the stems
in due time, according to rules and regulations
especially conferred upon the plants by the Creator.

Hand of the Cause A.Q. Faizi

Change is an evolutionary process requiring
patience with one's self and others, loving education
and the passage of time . . .

The Universal House of Justice[11]

A youth said to his father: 'O wise man,
Give me for instruction one advice
like an aged person.'
He said: 'Be kind but not to such a degree
That a sharp-toothed wolf may
become audacious.'

Gulistan[12]

It behoveth thee to nurture them at the breast of the love of God, and urge them onward to the things of the spirit . . .

'Abdu'l-Bahá[13]

The father must always endeavour to educate his son and to acquaint him with the heavenly teachings. He must give advice and exhort him at all times, teach him praiseworthy conduct and character, enable him to receive training at school and to be instructed in such arts and sciences as are deemed useful and necessary. In brief, let him instil into his mind the virtues and perfections of the world of humanity. Above all he should continually call to his mind the remembrance of God so that his throbbing veins and arteries may pulsate with the love of God.

The son, on the other hand, must show forth the utmost obedience towards his father, and should conduct himself as a humble and a lowly servant. Day and night he should seek diligently to ensure the comfort and welfare of his loving father and to secure his good-pleasure. He must forgo his own rest and enjoyment and constantly strive to bring gladness to the hearts of his father and mother, that thereby he may attain the good-pleasure of the Almighty and be graciously aided by the hosts of the unseen.

'Abdu'l-Bahá[14]

. . . it is incumbent on every one to send a child to school, and to teach it something. Because every duty and good work that a child performs is just as though the father and mother had performed it with their own hands. Therefore it is necessary to make an effort, so that they may teach them something good, and make them aware of good works and sin; for they are doing that on account of their own souls, so that those children may be courageous in doing good works.

If they are not taught, they then perform less duty and good works, and less reaches the souls of the father and mother. And it also happens that if they do not deliver children to school, and do not teach them anything, and they become bold in committing sin, that sin becomes fixed on the necks of the father and mother.

Sad Dar[15]

The stories of one's ancestors make the children good children. They accept what is pleasing to the Will of the True Guru, and act accordingly.

9 Shalok, Third Mehl

Do not confine your children to your own learning, for they were born in another time.

Hebrew Proverb

Fathers and Their Families

Families are where we first learn to
trust other people.

Jonathan Sacks[1]

And he dreamed, and behold a ladder set up on
the earth, and the top of it reached to heaven: and
behold the angels of God ascending and descending
on it. And, behold, the LORD stood above it, and
said, I am the lord God of Abraham thy father, and
the God of Isaac: the land whereon thou liest, to
thee will I give it, and to thy seed; And thy seed
shall be as the dust of the earth, and thou shalt
spread abroad to the west, and to the east, and to the
north, and to the south: and in thee and in thy seed
shall all the families of the earth be blessed.

Genesis 28: 12–14

. . . the unity of your family should take priority
over any other consideration. Bahá'u'lláh came to
bring unity to the world, and a fundamental unity is
that of the family.

On behalf of the Universal House of Justice[2]

A wise son maketh a glad father . . .

Proverbs 15:20

A foolish son is the calamity of his father . . .

Proverbs 19:13

By sharing good times a family builds cohesiveness
and unity. They learn to enjoy each other and
compensate for each other's weaknesses. The play
of children is something of a rehearsal for life, and
parents who share these times of play will have a
great opportunity to teach their children how to live.

Wayne Rickerson[3]

Note ye how easily, where unity existeth in a given
family, the affairs of that family are conducted; what
progress the members of that family make, how they
prosper in the world. Their concerns are in order,
they enjoy comfort and tranquillity, they are secure,
their position is assured, they come to be envied
by all. Such a family but added to its stature and its
lasting honour, as day succeedeth day . . .

'Abdu'l-Bahá[4]

Families are the crucible of our humanity. They
are the miniature world in which we learn how to
face the wider world. Strong families beget strong
individuals, people able to confront the future
without fear . . . For good or bad, the family is the
seedbed of the future. Stability and love are its sun
and rain. It is the best way we have yet found of
replacing insecurity with trust and making love the
generative principle of life.

Jonathan Sacks[5]

According to the teachings of Bahá'u'lláh the
family, being a human unit, must be educated
according to the rules of sanctity. All the virtues
must be taught the family. The integrity of the
family bond must be constantly considered, and
the rights of the individual members must not be
transgressed. The rights of the son, the father, the
mother – none of them must be transgressed, none
of them must be arbitrary. Just as the son has certain
obligations to his father, the father, likewise, has
certain obligations to his son. The mother, the sister
and other members of the household have their
certain prerogatives. All these rights and prerogatives
must be conserved, yet the unity of the family must
be sustained. The injury of one shall be considered
the injury of all; the comfort of each, the comfort of
all; the honour of one, the honour of all.

'Abdu'l-Bahá[6]

The father of the righteous shall greatly rejoice:
      and he that begetteth a wise child shall
      have joy of him.
Thy father and thy mother shall be glad, and she
      that bare thee shall rejoice.
My son, give me thine heart, and let thine eyes
      observe my ways.

Proverbs 23:24–6

Whoso keepeth the law is a wise son . . .

Proverbs 28:7

The members of a family all have duties and
responsibilities towards one another and to
the family as a whole, and these duties and
responsibilities vary from member to member
because of their natural relationships. The parents
have the inescapable duty to educate their children
– but not vice versa; the children have the duty to
obey their parents – the parents do not obey the
children; the mother – not the father – bears the
children, nurses them in babyhood, and is thus their
first educator; hence daughters have a prior right to
education over sons . . .

The Universal House of Justice[7]

In the family I learn the complex choreography of
love – what it means to give and take and share,
to grow from obedience to responsibility, to learn,
challenge, rebel, make mistakes, to forgive and be
forgiven, to argue and make up, to win without
triumph and know when to lose graciously. It
is where we acquire emotional intelligence, that
delicate negotiation between the given and the
chosen, the things I will and the things resistant to
my will.

Jonathan Sacks[8]

Husbands, love your wives, and be not bitter against them. Children, obey your parents in all things: for this is well pleasing unto the Lord. Fathers, provoke not your children to anger, lest they be discouraged.

Colossians 3:19–21

God has always intended that values be communicated through the family in an atmosphere of family love. Godly values are not passed on from parents to children in a vacuum. They grow in an atmosphere of healthy interaction and are based on good relationships between parents and children. The only way that relationships are built within a family is by time spent together.

Wayne Rickerson[9]

I have always been a rich man. I have my family and we have our good health. We have land to farm, houses to live in, food on our tables, and enough clothes. Most of all, we have the love in our hearts for each other and our friends.

Tsali, Cherokee[10]

Children are the reward of life.

Congolese Proverb

A man with many children has many homes.

Lakota Proverb[11]

Through love as the bond between parents and
children we understand the love of God for
mankind. Through the trust that grows in families,
we discover what it is to have trust in God and in
His world.

Jonathan Sacks[12]

In reality, children are the ornaments at the table,
especially these children, who are very sweet! The
hearts of children are extremely pure and simple. A
person's heart must be like a child's, pure and free
from all contamination.

'Abdu'l-Bahá[13]

Families matter in all sorts of way. Children are
among the most vulnerable members of society.
How we treat them is one of the best measures of
the kind of people we are. Children have fared
badly in our affluent world. They have less of their
parents' time and attention, less security at home,
than a generation or two ago. A mountain of
research has counted the cost. Children today are
more prone to depression, anxiety, suicidal feelings,
drug and alcohol abuse, violence and crime than at
any point in recent times. What kind of adult world
is it that indulges itself and neglects its children?

No less scandalous are the myths we have
invented to justify all this: that 'quality time' makes
up for lack of time; that child care is the same as

parental care; that what we cannot give, we can
pay others to give; that all sorts of families – dual
parent or single parent, stable or fractured, lasting or
temporary, male-female or single sex – are the same
in their effects upon a child. No future generation
will understand how we convinced ourselves that we
really believed these things.

Jonathan Sacks[14]

For the Lord hath given the father honour over the
children, and hath confirmed the authority of the
mother over the sons.

Sirach 3:2

> In dwelling, live close to the ground.
> In thinking, keep to the simple.
> In conflict, be fair and generous.
> In governing, don't try to control.
> In work, do what you enjoy.
> In family life, be completely present.
>
> When you are content to be simply yourself
> and don't compare or compete,
> everybody will respect you.

Tao te Ching

Like a son following his father's wishes, grant
      to this family success and safety.

Soma Pavamana[15]

If love and agreement are manifest in a single family, that family will advance, become illumined and spiritual . . .

'Abdu'l-Bahá[16]

Fathers and the Home

Blessed is the spot, and the house . . .
where mention of God hath been made,
and His praise glorified.

Bahá'u'lláh[1]

The upbuilding of a home, the bringing of joy
and comfort into human hearts are truly glories
of mankind.

'Abdu'l-Bahá[2]

Unto thee, O God, we dedicate this home. Cleanse
it from all that is alien to Thee that it may become
fit for Thy acceptance, and may be to friend and
stranger as to ourselves a place of peace, a refuge
from materialism, a herald of Thy Kingdom.

George Townshend[3]

This home is a garden, O Lord, which Thy hand
has planted in the world, and the hearts of these
children are Thy flowers. Do Thou tend them and
nourish them.

Pour down the rays of Thy truth upon them.
Breathe Thy Holy Spirit upon them at every breath.
Let Thy mercy descend on them like refreshing rain.

So shall these flowers of Thine mature, and
bloom in beauty, and shed afar the fragrance of Thy
love and remain thine to their lives' end.

George Townshend[4]

Together make mention of noble aspirations and heavenly concepts. Let there be no secrets one from another. Make your house a haven of rest and peace. Be hospitable, and let the doors of your house be open to the faces of friends and strangers. Welcome every guest with radiant grace and let each feel that it is his own home . . .

O beloved of God, may your home be a vision of the paradise of Abhá, so that whosoever enters there may feel the essence of purity and harmony, and cry out from the heart: 'Here is the home of love! Here is the palace of love! Here is the nest of love! Here is the garden of love!'

Attributed to 'Abdu'l-Bahá[5]

The householder who gives in charity all he can afford is as pure as the waters of the Ganga.

Sikh Scriptures[6]

. . . thou art like unto a melodious nightingale, singing and warbling in the rose-garden of the love of God, and art uttering of the mystery of the Kingdom . . . thy house and dwelling is a meeting-place of the spiritual ones and thy nest and abode is a shelter for the birds of heaven. Nothing is better than that man should become a manifestor of the powers of God and the cause of illuminating the creatures.

'Abdu'l-Bahá[7]

The Story of San'hode'di'begaeye, the Beggar's Son

> I am the White Corn Boy.
> I walk in sight of my home.
> I walk in plain sight of my home.
> I walk on the straight path which is
>   towards my home.
> I walk to the entrance of my home.
> I arrive at the beautiful goods curtain
>   which hangs at the doorway.
> I arrive at the entrance of my home.
> I am in the middle of my home.
> I am at the back of my home.
> I am on top of the pollen foot print.
> I am on top of the pollen seed print.
> I am like the Most High Power Whose
>   Ways Are Beautiful.
> Before me it is beautiful,
> Behind me it is beautiful,
> Under me it is beautiful,
> Above me it is beautiful,
> All around me it is beautiful.

Thou art be whose home is right, whose light is the
heaven. Thou art be whose light is the Brahman,
whose home is the heaven.

Prapathaka[8]

. . . make thou thy meetings a palace for the
heavenly beloved and thy residence a glass for the
light of Deity. Suffer thy home to become a nest for
the dove of the Holy Spirit and thine eye the mirror
for the reflection of the Beauty of the Almighty.

'Abdu'l-Bahá[9]

. . . turn thee homeward; thy joy is in thy home . . .

Rig Veda[10]

He who knows the home, becomes a home of his
people. The mind indeed is the home.

Khandogya-Upanishad[11]

Where is my home, O Jehovah! When I was happy
          and my feet wandered.
I dwelt with Thy hosts, afar! afar! Thy glory shining.
O the songs in Thy upraised kingdoms! when shall I
          rejoice in the music of my own house?
O those sparkling, running waters? O the pastimes
          and feasts of love!
Where is it, O Jehovah? It was my home in high
          heaven!
I fell, I fell in darkness! Wandering soul within me,
          that ledest me forth.
The gardens of Jehovah stood on every hand. O
          senseless feet to take me onward!
Into the darkness was I lured; sweet perfumes rose
          amidst the darkness.

Intricate in Thy glory, O Jehovah! I lost the way. I
was lost!
The music of Thy spheres was shut out. I was
environed in darkness!
Where is my home, O Jehovah? Why have I
forsaken it?
Crystals, and high arches on every hand. Full,
standing out, shining.
And the songs of my sweet loves! Such was my
home and place of revelry!
I bartered them all away, wandering forth. Buried
me in the opaque, in the dark!
O for my home in high heaven! Mirth, song, rest,
and love, clear shining.
Thou, O Jehovah, hast given me sons and daughters.
Out of this darkness my gems were born!
O I will polish them up. Kin of my kin, I will raise
them up!
Thy Goddesses in heaven above will come. In ships
of fire descending!
My jewels shall enter and rise with me. We shall
search for my home; the haven of rest!
I see Thee, O Jehovah, afar off. Higher than the
highest of heavens!
O hasten, my home, and my rest! O ripen these, my
precious diadems!
O take us to ethereal worlds.

Book of Sethantes 4:8–29

O Maker of the material world, thou Holy one!
Which is the second place where the Earth feels
most happy? Ahura Mazda answered: 'It is the place
whereon one of the faithful erects a house with a
priest within, with cattle, with a wife, with children,
and good herds within; and wherein afterwards the
cattle continue to thrive, virtue to thrive, fodder to
thrive, the dog to thrive, the wife to thrive, the child
to thrive, the fire to thrive, and every blessing of life
to thrive.'

The Earth, Fargard 3[12]

. . . it is thy duty to protect thy home, thy wife, thy
children, and thy children's children against the
hurtful influences of evil spirits . . .

To guard thy home by mysterious ceremonies is
not sufficient; thou must guard it by good deeds.
Turn to thy parents in the East, to thy teachers in
the South, to thy wife and children in the West, to
thy friends in the North, and regulate the zenith
of thy religious relations above thee, and the nadir
of thy servants below thee. Such is the religion thy
father wants thee to have . . .

Guard the Six Quarters

Children are the ornaments of the home. A home
which has no children is like one without light.

'Abdu'l-Bahá[13]

Father's Story

We put more coal on the big fire,
     And while we are waiting for dinner to cook,
Our father comes and tells us about
     A story that he has read in a book.

And Charles and Will and Dick and I
     And all of us but Clarence are there.
And some of us sit on Father's legs,
     But one has to sit on the little red chair.

And when we are sitting very still,
     He sings us a song or tells a piece;
He sings 'Dan Tucker Went to Town',
     Or he tells us about the golden fleece.

He tells us about the golden wool,
     And some of it is about a boy
Named Jason, and about a ship,
     And some is about a town called Troy.

And while he is telling or singing it through,
     I stand by his arm, for that is my place,
And I push my fingers into his skin
     To make little dents in his big round face.
Elizabeth Madox Roberts

What the child says, he has heard at home.
Nigerian Proverb

Home is where
the heart can find
comfort, pleasure
peace of mind.

Anon.

Honour Thy Father

Verily, We have enjoined on every son
to serve his father.

Baháʼuʼlláh[1]

O dear one of ʻAbduʼl-Bahá! Be the son of thy father
and be the fruit of that tree. Be a son that hath been
born of his soul and heart and not only of water
and clay. A real son is such a one as hath branched
from the spiritual part of man. I ask God that thou
mayest be at all times confirmed and strengthened.

ʻAbduʼl-Bahá[2]

O ye dear children!

Your father is compassionate, clement and
merciful unto you and desireth for you success,
prosperity and eternal life in the Kingdom of God.
Therefore, it is incumbent upon you, dear children,
to seek his good pleasure, to be guided by his
guidance, to be drawn by the magnet of the
love of God and be brought up in the lap of the love
of God; that ye may become beautiful branches in
the Gardens of El-Abhá, verdant and watered by the
abundance of the gift of God.

ʻAbduʼl-Bahá[3]

It is incumbent upon the youth to walk in the
footsteps of Ḥakím and to be trained in his
ways . . . The youth must grow and develop and
take the place of their fathers, that this abundant

grace, in the posterity of each one of the loved ones of God who bore great agonies, may day by day increase, until in the end it shall yield its fruit on earth and in Heaven.

'Abdu'l-Bahá[4]

Children, obey your parents in the Lord: for this is right. Honour thy father and mother; which is the first commandment with promise; That it may be well with thee, and thou mayest live long on the earth. And, ye fathers, provoke not your children to wrath: but bring them up in the nurture and admonition of the Lord.

Ephesians 6: 1–4

My son, hear the instruction of thy father, and forsake not the law of thy mother: For they shall be an ornament of grace unto thy head, and chains about thy neck.

Proverbs 1:8–9

Thy wish is to serve thy father, who is dear to thee, and also to serve the Kingdom of God, and thou art perplexed as to which of the two thou shouldst do. Assuredly engage in service to thy father, and as well, whenever thou findest time, diffuse the divine fragrances.

'Abdu'l-Bahá[5]

The aged should be respected and revered. He who does this will receive great rewards and will prosper. Children should give support to their parents. One should always honour one's parents.

Buddhist Scripture[6]

Appreciate the value of thy father, for he taught thee to await the manifestation of the Light of Lights. Verily he hath inhaled the fragrance of the Paradise of El-Abhá and his nostrils are therewith perfumed. Therefore, he bade thee to anticipate and prepare thyself for the appearance of the Kingdom of God.

'Abdu'l-Bahá[7]

Whoso honoureth his father maketh an atonement
for his sins:
And he that honoureth his mother is as one that
layeth up treasure.
Whoso honoureth his father shall have joy of his
own children; and when he maketh his
prayer, he shall be heard.
He that honoureth his father shall have a long life;
and he that is obedient unto the Lord shall
be a comfort to his mother.
He that feareth the Lord will honour his father, and
will do service unto his parents, as to his
masters.

Honour thy father and mother both in word and
        deed, that a blessing may come upon thee
        from them.
For the blessing of the father establisheth the houses
        of children . . .
Glory not in the dishonour of thy father; for thy
        father's dishonour is no glory unto thee.
For the glory of a man is from the honour of
        his father . . .
My son, help thy father in his age, and grieve him
        not as long as he liveth.
And if his understanding fail, have patience with
        him; and despise him not when thou art in
        thy full strength.
For the relieving of thy father shall not be forgotten:
        and instead of sins it shall be added to build
        thee up.
In the day of thine affliction it shall be remembered;
        thy sins also shall melt away, as the ice in the
        fair warm weather.
He that forsaketh his father is as a blasphemer;
        and he that angereth his mother is cursed
        of God.
My son, go on with thy business in meekness;
        so shalt thou be beloved of him that is
        approved.
The greater thou art, the more humble thyself, and
        thou shalt find favour before the Lord.

Sirach 3:3–18

Honour thy father with thy whole heart,
and forget not the sorrows of thy mother.

Sirach 7:27

Remember thy father and thy mother, when thou
sittest among great men. Be not forgetful before
them, and so thou by thy custom become a fool,
and wish that thou hadst not been born, and curse
the day of thy nativity.

Sirach 23:14

Honour thy father and thy mother, as the LORD thy
God hath commanded thee; that thy days may be
prolonged, and that it may go well with thee, in the
land which the LORD thy God giveth thee.

Deuteronomy 5:16

Living with Brahma are those families where, in
the home, mother and father are revered by the
children. Living with the first devas are those
families where, in the home, mother and father
are revered by the children. Living with the first
teachers are those families where, in the home,
mother and father are revered by the children.
Living with those worthy of gifts are those families
where, in the home, mother and father are revered
by the children. 'Brahma' is a designation for
mother and father. 'The first devas' is a designation
for mother and father. 'The first teachers' is a

designation for mother and father. 'Those worthy of gifts' is a designation for mother and father. Why is that? Mother and father do much for their children. They care for them, nourish them, introduce them to this world.

Mother & father
    compassionate to their family
    are called
    Brahma,
        the first teachers
        those worthy of gifts from their
        children.
    So the sage should pay them
            homage
            honour
        with food and drink
        clothing and bedding
        anointing and bathing
        and washing their feet.
    Performing these services to their parents,
    the wise
        are praised here and now
        and after death
        rejoice in heaven.

Itivuttaka 4[8]

Thou dost well, O Sigala, to honour, reverence, and keep sacred the words of thy father . . .

Guard the Six Quarters

Towards a mother (grandmother and great-grandmother) and a father (grandfather and great-grandfather) the same obedience must be shown as towards a teacher.

Âpastamba Prasna I°

On the principle of gratefulness, we support our parents and serve them filially.

The Sutra of Hui Neng

Fathers' Sacrifices

Behold a candle how it gives its light.
It weeps its life away drop by drop in
order to give forth its flame of light.

'Abdu'l-Bahá[1]

The wise man works not for the present moment but
for the good results of the future.

'Abdu'l-Bahá[2]

It is true that children are expensive, time-
consuming, patience-taxing additions to the family,
but the sacrifices they demand are trivial to what
they give.

Chad Walsh

Nothing in life just happens. You have to have the
stamina to meet the obstacles and overcome them.

Golda Meir

Enjoy the little things, for one day you may look
back and realize they were the big things.

Robert Brault

Anyone can hold the helm when the sea is calm.

Publius Syrus

The art of being a parent consists of sleeping when
the baby isn't looking.

Anon

It now costs more to amuse a child than it once did to educate his father.

Vaughan Monroe

Those who bring sunshine to the lives of others cannot keep it from themselves.

James Matthew Barrie

We can do no great things –
only small things with great love.

Mother Teresa

Without some goal and some effort to reach it, no man can live.

Feodor Dostoevsky

. . . we are worth what we are willing
to share with others.

Sir Moses Montifiore

The hardest struggle of all is to be something different from what the average man is.

Charles M. Schwab

The way I see it, if you want the rainbow, you gotta put up with the rain.

Dolly Parton

He who wants pearls has to dive into the sea.
Kurdish Proverb

Love

Love is the Portal to Freedom.
Howard Colby Ives[1]

. . . when the heart is filled with love everything
seems beautiful and delightful to us.
'Abdu'l-Bahá[2]

Love is very patient and kind, never jealous or
envious, never boastful or proud, never haughty or
selfish or rude. Love does not demand its own way.
It is not irritable or touchy. It does not hold grudges
and will hardly even notice when others do it wrong.
It is never glad about injustice, but rejoices whenever
truth wins out. If you love someone, you will be
loyal to him no matter what the cost. You will
always believe in him, always expect the best of him,
and always stand your ground in defending him.
I Corinthians 13:4–7

Know thou of a certainty that Love is the secret of
God's holy Dispensation, the manifestation of the
All-Merciful, the fountain of spiritual outpourings.
Love is heaven's kindly light, the Holy Spirit's
eternal breath that vivifieth the human soul. Love
is the cause of God's revelation unto man, the
vital bond inherent, in accordance with the divine
creation, in the realities of things. Love is the
one means that ensureth true felicity both in this
world and the next. Love is the light that guideth

in darkness, the living link that uniteth God with
man, that assureth the progress of every illumined
soul. Love is the most great law that ruleth this
mighty and heavenly cycle, the unique power that
bindeth together the divers elements of this material
world, the supreme magnetic force that directeth the
movements of the spheres in the celestial realms.
Love revealeth with unfailing and limitless power
the mysteries latent in the universe. Love is the
spirit of life unto the adorned body of mankind, the
establisher of true civilization in this mortal world,
and the shedder of imperishable glory upon every
high-aiming race and nation.

'Abdu'l-Bahá[3]

Love understands all languages.
                    Romanian Proverb

Love is the communication between truth and man
in the realm of consciousness.

'Abdu'l-Bahá[4]

Love is not blind – it sees more, not less. But
because it sees more, it is willing to see less.
                    Rabbi Julius Gordon

All loves should be simply stepping stones
            to the love of God.

Plato

Love begets love.

M. Scott Peck[5]

When you love a member of your family . . . let it be with a ray of the Infinite Love! Let it be in God, and for God! Wherever you find the attributes of God love that person, whether he be of your family or of another. Shed the light of a boundless love on every human being whom you meet . . .

'Abdu'l-Bahá[6]

Love gives life to the lifeless. Love lights a flame in the heart that is cold. Love brings hope to the hopeless and gladdens the hearts of the sorrowful.

'Abdu'l-Bahá[7]

The more I love, the longer I love, the larger I become. Genuine love is self-replenishing. The more I nurture the spiritual growth of others, the more my own spiritual growth is nurtured.

M. Scott Peck[8]

. . . we *must* convey our love to our children *before anything else*: before teaching, before guidance, before example, before discipline. Unconditional love must be the basic relationship with a child . . .

Ross Campbell[9]

By the accident of good fortune a man may rule the
world for a time. But by the virtue of love he may
rule the world for ever.

Philosophy of Tao

The love of one's children and spouse
is so sweet in this world.

Sikh Scriptures

Love will teach us all things: but we must learn how
to win love; it is got with difficulty; it is a possession
dearly bought with much labour and a long time;
for one must love not sometimes only, for a passing
moment, but always. There is no man who doth not
sometimes love: even the wicked can do that. And
let no men's sin dishearten thee: love a man even
in his sin, for that love is a likeness of the divine
love, and is the summit of love on earth. Love all
God's creation, both the whole and every grain of
sand. Love every leaf, every ray of light. Love the
animals, love the plants, love each separate thing. If
thou love each thing thou wilt perceive the mystery
of God in all: and when once thou perceive this,
thou wilt henceforward grow every day to a fuller
understanding of it: until thou hast come at last to
love the whole world with a love that will then be
all-embracing and universal.

Feodor Dostoevsky

If your hearts are turned always toward God, and filled with the love of God, that love will separate them from all other things, that love will be the wall that will come between them and every other desire. You must be all joined one to another in heart and soul, then you will be prospered in your work and gain ever greater gifts . . .

Attributed to 'Abdu'l-Bahá[10]

Children must be trained through love.

Attributed to 'Abdu'l-Bahá[11]

Where there is love, there is happiness.

Polish Proverb

We cannot start too early in giving a child continuous, warm, consistent affection. He simply *must* have this unconditional love to cope most effectively in today's world.

Ross Campbell[12]

Ultimately love is everything.

M. Scott Peck[13]

Spiritual Qualities

Joy is the echo of God's life within us.
Joseph Marmion

If a man lives his life without joy, then death
would be better. True happiness and joy come from
composure of the heart, and this comes from faith.
'Abdu'l-Bahá[1]

The character of a man lies not in his body
but in his soul.
Japanese Proverb

Each life must find its own revelation of Religion, as
each life must find its own revelation of Love.
Marah Ellis Ryan

God does not want us to do extraordinary things; He
wants us to do ordinary things extraordinarily well.
Bishop Gore

The just man walketh in his integrity: his children
are blessed after him.

Proverbs 20:7

The goodness of the father reaches higher than
a mountain; that of the mother deeper than
the ocean.

Japanese Proverb

Help me today to realize that you will be speaking
to me through the events of the day, through
people, through things, and through all creation.
Give me ears, eyes and heart to perceive you,
however veiled your presence may be. Give me
insight to see through the exterior of things to the
interior truth. Give me your Spirit of discernment!
O Lord, thou knowest how busy I must be this day.
If I forget thee, do not forget me!

Jacob Astley

There can be no doubt whatever that, in
consequence of the efforts which every man may
consciously exert and as a result of the exertion of
his own spiritual faculties, this mirror can be so
cleansed from the dross of earthly defilements and
purged from satanic fancies as to be able to draw
nigh unto the meads of eternal holiness and attain
the courts of everlasting fellowship.

Bahá'u'lláh[2]

Say: Let truthfulness and courtesy be your adorning.
Suffer not yourselves to be deprived of the robe of
forbearance and justice, that the sweet savours of
holiness may be wafted from your hearts upon all
created things.

Bahá'u'lláh[3]

Keep your fears to yourself, but share your courage.
Robert Louis Stevenson

O Son of Glory! Be swift in the path of holiness,
and enter the heaven of communion with Me.
Cleanse thy heart with the burnish of the spirit, and
hasten to the court of the Most High.
Bahá'u'lláh[4]

If it be Thy pleasure, make me to grow as a tender
herb in the meadows of Thy grace, that the gentle
winds of Thy will may stir me up and bend me into
conformity with Thy pleasure, in such wise that my
movement and my stillness may be wholly directed
by Thee.
Bahá'u'lláh[5]

Ye are the stars of the heaven of understanding, the
breeze that stirreth at the break of day, the soft-
flowing waters upon which must depend the very
life of all men, the letters inscribed upon His
sacred scroll.
Bahá'u'lláh[6]

In the eyes of the All-Merciful a true man appeareth
even as a firmament; its sun and moon are his
sight and hearing, and his shining and resplendent
character its stars.
Bahá'u'lláh[7]

> Keep your face to the sunshine
> and you cannot see the shadow.
>   *Helen Keller*

Seek for spiritual joy and knowledge, then, though
thou walk upon this earth, thou wilt be dwelling
within the divine realm.

'Abdu'l-Bahá[8]

Bahá'u'lláh bore all these ordeals and catastrophes
        for this:
    That our hearts might be illumined.
    That our spirits might become glad.
    That our imperfections might be replaced
        by virtues.
    That our ignorance might be transformed
        into knowledge.
In order that we might acquire the fruits of
        humanity and obtain Heavenly graces.

'Abdu'l-Bahá[9]

A race of men, incomparable in character, shall be
raised up which, with the feet of detachment, will
tread under all who are in heaven and on earth, and
will cast the sleeve of holiness over all that hath
been created from water and clay.

Bahá'u'lláh[10]

Man's greatest privilege is to become a suitable instrument of God, and until he knows this he has not realized his true purpose.

Inayat Khan

Do not walk in God's ways on someone else's behalf.

Bambara Proverb

Everybody thinks of changing humanity and nobody thinks of changing himself.

Leo Tolstoy

Fathers: Establishers of Peace

How beautiful are the feet of them
that preach the gospel of peace, and bring
glad tidings of good things!

Romans 10:15

Thou must show forth that which will ensure the
peace and the well-being of the miserable and the
downtrodden.

Bahá'u'lláh[1]

Better than if there were thousands
of meaningless words is
one meaningful word
that on hearing
brings peace.

Better than if there were thousands
of meaningless verses is
one meaningful verse
that on hearing
brings peace.

And better than chanting hundreds
of meaningless verses is one
Dhamma-saying
that on hearing
brings peace.

Dhammapada, Thousands

And into whatsoever house ye enter, first say, Peace
be to this house. And if the son of peace be there,
your peace shall rest upon it: if not, it shall turn to
you again.

Luke 10:5–6

We ask God, exalted be His glory, to confirm each
one of the friends in that land in the acquisition of
such praiseworthy characteristics as shall conduce
to the spread of justice and equity among the
peoples of the world. The first, the fundamental
purpose underlying creation hath ever been, and
will continue to be, none other than the appearance
of trustworthiness and godliness, of sincerity and
goodwill amongst mankind, for these qualities are
the cause of peace, security and tranquillity. Blessed
are those who possess such virtues.

Bahá'u'lláh[2]

Nothing can bring you peace but
the triumph of principles.
Ralph Waldo Emerson

As long as a person does not know the richness of
joy and peace that comes from within, he tries to fill
his empty and insecure existence with the clutter of
material acquisitions.

Jain Scriptures[3]

Be thou severed from this world, and reborn
through the sweet scents of holiness that blow from
the realm of the All-Highest. Be thou a summoner
to love, and be thou kind to all the human race.
Love thou the children of men and share in their
sorrows. Be thou of those who foster peace. Offer
thy friendship, be worthy of trust. Be thou a balm
to every sore, be thou a medicine for every ill. Bind
thou the souls together. Recite thou the verses of
guidance. Be engaged in the worship of thy Lord,
and rise up to lead the people aright. Loose thy
tongue and teach, and let thy face be bright with
the fire of God's love. Rest thou not for a moment,
seek thou to draw no easeful breath. Thus mayest
thou become a sign and symbol of God's love, and a
banner of His grace.

'Abdu'l-Bahá[4]

Let thy sons and Pandu's children stand beside
       thy ancient throne,
Cherish peace and cherish virtue, for thy days
       are almost done!

Krishna's Speech at Hastina, Mahabharata

. . . there can never be peace between nations until
there is first known that true peace which . . . is
within the souls of men.

Black Elk[5]

One can never be sincere enough until his heart is
entirely severed from attachment to the things of
this world. One should not preach love and have
a loveless heart, nor preach purity and harbour
impure thoughts. Nor preach peace and be at
inward strife.

Attributed to 'Abdu'l-Bahá[6]

Listen to my friendly counsel – though it be
      I stand alone –
  Faithful friend but fiery foeman is this
        Dasa-ratha's son,
Listen to my voice of warning – Rama's shafts
      are true and keen,
  Flaming like the with'ring sunbeams on the
        summer's parchéd green,
Listen to my soft entreaty – righteousness
      becomes the brave,
  Cherish peace and cherish virtue and thy
        sons and daughters save!

Bibhishan's Warning, Mahabharata

We have exhorted them at length in various Tablets
and beseech God to graciously assist them, to enable
them to draw nigh unto Him and to confirm them
in that which would bring peace to the hearts and
tranquillity to the souls . . .

Bahá'u'lláh[7]

A disciplined person, enjoying sense objects
with senses that are under control and free from
attachments and aversions, attains tranquillity.

All sorrows are destroyed upon attainment of
tranquillity. The intellect of such a tranquil person
soon becomes completely steady and united with
the Supreme. There is neither Self-knowledge, nor
Self-perception to those who are not united with the
Supreme.

Without Self-perception there is no peace, and
without peace there can be no happiness. Because
the mind, when controlled by the roving senses,
steals away the intellect as a storm takes away a boat
on the sea from its destination – the spiritual shore
of peace and happiness.

Therefore, O Arjuna, one's intellect becomes
steady whose senses are completely withdrawn from
the sense objects . . .

One attains peace, within whose mind all desires
dissipate without creating any mental disturbance,
as river waters enter the full ocean without creating
any disturbance. One who desires material objects is
never peaceful.

One who abandons all desires, and becomes free
from longing and the feeling of 'I' and 'my', attains
peace.

Bhagavad Gita[8]

O Lord God, grant us thy peace – for thou hast
given us all things. Grant us the peace of quietness,
the peace of the Sabbath, the peace without an
evening. All this most beautiful array of things, all
so very good, will pass away when all their courses
are finished – for in them there is both morning
and evening.

St Augustine[9]

The sage asked the spirit of wisdom thus: 'Which is
that good work which is greater and better than all
good works, and no trouble whatever is necessary for
its performance?'

The spirit of wisdom answered thus: 'To be
grateful in the world, and to wish happiness for
every one. This is greater and better than every good
work, and no commotion whatever is necessary for
its performance.'

Peace and prosperity.

Menog-i Khrad[10]

Today there is no greater glory for man than that of
service in the cause of the Most Great Peace. Peace
is light, whereas war is darkness. Peace is life; war is
death. Peace is guidance; war is error. Peace is the
foundation of God; war is a satanic institution. Peace
is the illumination of the world of humanity; war
is the destroyer of human foundations. When we
consider outcomes in the world of existence, we find

that peace and fellowship are factors of upbuilding
and betterment, whereas war and strife are the
causes of destruction and disintegration. All created
things are expressions of the affinity and cohesion
of elementary substances, and nonexistence is the
absence of their attraction and agreement. Various
elements unite harmoniously in composition, but
when these elements become discordant, repelling
each other, decomposition and nonexistence result.
Everything partakes of this nature and is subject to
this principle, for the creative foundation in all its
degrees and kingdoms is an expression or outcome
of love. Consider the restlessness and agitation of the
human world today because of war. Peace is health
and construction; war is disease and dissolution.
When the banner of truth is raised, peace becomes
the cause of the welfare and advancement of the
human world. In all cycles and ages war has been a
factor of derangement and discomfort, whereas peace
and brotherhood have brought security . . .

'Abdu'l-Bahá[11]

O brother man, hold to thy heart thy brother;
Where pity dwells, the peace of God is there; To
worship rightly is to love each other; Each smile a
hymn, each kindly word a prayer.

John Greenleaf Whittier

From the monarch's ancient bosom sighs and sobs
      convulsive broke,
Bhishma wiped his manly eyelids and to proud
      Duryodhan spoke:
      'Listen, prince, for righteous Krishna
            counsels love and holy peace,
      Listen, youth, and may thy fortune with thy
            passing years increase!
      Yield to Krishna's words of wisdom, for thy
            weal he nobly strives,
      Yield and save thy friends and kinsmen, save
            thy cherished subjects' lives . . .
               Bhishma's Speech, Mahabharata

Make haste to love! Make haste to trust! Make haste
to give! To guidance come!

    Come ye for harmony! To behold the Star of
Day! Come here for kindliness, for ease! Come here
for amity and peace!

    Come and cast down your weapons of wrath, till
unity is won! Come and in the Lord's true path each
one help each one.

                   'Abdu'l-Bahá[12]

Let us therefore follow after the things which make
for peace . . .

                      Romans 14:19

I charge you all that each one of you concentrate
all the thoughts of your heart on love and unity.
When a thought of war comes, oppose it by a
stronger thought of peace. A thought of hatred must
be destroyed by a more powerful thought of love.
Thoughts of war bring destruction to all harmony,
well-being, restfulness and content.

Thoughts of love are constructive of brother-
hood, peace, friendship, and happiness.

'Abdu'l-Bahá[13]

Strive for universal peace, seek the means of love,
and destroy the basis of disagreement so that this
material world may become divine, the world of
matter become the realm of the Kingdom and
humanity attain to the world of perfection.

'Abdu'l-Bahá[14]

If the learned and worldly-wise men of this age
were to allow mankind to inhale the fragrance of
fellowship and love, every understanding heart
would apprehend the meaning of true liberty,
and discover the secret of undisturbed peace and
absolute composure. Were the earth to attain this
station and be illumined with its light it could then
be truly said of it: 'Thou shall see in it no hollows or
rising hills.'

Bahá'u'lláh[15]

My son, forget not my law; but let thine heart
keep my commandments: For length of days, and
long life, and peace, shall they add to thee. Let not
mercy and truth forsake thee: bind them about thy
neck; write them upon the table of thine heart: So
shalt thou find favour and good understanding
in the sight of God and man. Trust in the LORD
with all thine heart; and lean not unto thine own
understanding. In all thy ways acknowledge him,
and he shall direct thy paths.

Proverbs 3:1–6

Let us pray for eyes to see and ears to hear, and for
hearts that long for peace.

'Abdu'l-Bahá[16]

O Vastospati, accept us; Be of kind entrance for us
and free from ill; That which we seek from thee, do
thou accord us, And health be thou for our bipeds,
health for our quadrupeds. O Vastospati, may we be
comrades of thee. In a friendship, effectual, joyful,
and proceeding well; Aid our wishes in peace, in
action; Do ye guard us ever with blessings.

Prapathaka IV[17]

May for me prosperity, comfort, desire, wish,
longing, kindliness, good, better, superior, fame,
good luck, riches, restrainer, supporter, peace,
firmness, all, greatness, discovery, knowledge,

begetting, procreation, plough, harrow, holy
order, immortality, freeness from disease, freedom
from illness, life, longevity, freedom from foes,
fearlessness, ease of going, lying, fair dawning, and
fair day (prosper through the sacrifice).

Prapathaka VII[18]

I think that people want peace so much that one of
these days, governments had better get out of the
way and let them have it.

Dwight D. Eisenhower

Men of the New World Order

The world's equilibrium hath been upset through the vibrating influence of this most great, this new World Order. Mankind's ordered life hath been revolutionized through the agency of this unique, this wondrous System – the like of which mortal eyes have never witnessed.

Bahá'u'lláh[1]

I find the great thing in this world is not so much where we stand as in what direction we are moving.

Oliver Wendell Holmes

A seed in the beginning is very small, but in the end a great tree. One should not consider the seed, but the tree and its abundance of blossoms, leaves and fruits.

'Abdu'l-Bahá[2]

The most difficult mountain to
cross is the threshold.

Danish Proverb

When I was young, I wanted to change the world. I tried, but the world didn't change. Then I decided to change my town, but the town didn't change. Then I tried to change my family, but my family didn't change. Then I realized: first, I must change myself.

Rabbi Yisrael Salanter[3]

The principle of the equality between women
and men . . . can be effectively and universally
established among the friends when it is pursued
in conjunction with all the other aspects of Bahá'í
life. Change is an evolutionary process requiring
patience with one's self and others, loving education
and the passage of time as the believers deepen
their knowledge of the principles of the Faith,
gradually discard long-held traditional attitudes and
progressively conform their lives to the unifying
teachings of the Cause.

On behalf of the Universal House of Justice[4]

The happiness of mankind will be realized when
women and men coordinate and advance equally,
for each is the complement and helpmeet of
the other.

'Abdu'l-Bahá[5]

Ere long the days shall come when the men
addressing the women, shall say: 'Blessed are ye!
Blessed are ye! Verily ye are worthy of every gift.
Verily ye deserve to adorn your heads with the
crown of everlasting glory, because in sciences and
arts, in virtues and perfections ye shall become
equal to man, and as regards tenderness of heart
and the abundance of mercy and sympathy ye
are superior.'

'Abdu'l-Bahá[6]

Change starts when someone sees the next step.
William Drayton

And let it be known once more that until woman
and man recognize and realize equality, social
and political progress here or anywhere will not be
possible. For the world of humanity consists of two
parts or members: one is woman; the other is man.
Until these two members are equal in strength, the
oneness of humanity cannot be established, and
the happiness and felicity of mankind will not be a
reality. God willing, this is to be so.
'Abdu'l-Bahá[7]

As long as women are prevented from attaining their
highest possibilities, so long will men be unable to
achieve the greatness which might be theirs.
'Abdu'l-Bahá[8]

When men own the equality of women there will be
no need for them to struggle for their rights!
'Abdu'l-Bahá[9]

My interest is in the future . . . because I'm
going to spend the rest of my life there.
Charles Kettering

. . . with eyes of faith look into the future, for in truth the Spirit of God is working in your midst.

'Abdu'l-Bahá[10]

It is as odd to say that humans need roots as to say they need foliage. But a generation which values adaptability as much as tradition, which seeks energy and creativity and openness of mind, must like the idea of drinking in the light of the sun, from whatever direction it shines. And applied to humans, this means that it is not just where they come from that matters, but where they are going, what kind of curiosity or imagination they have, and how they use it, both by day and by night.

Theodore Zeldin

In the long run what any society is to become will depend upon what it believes or disbelieves about the eternal things.

Bishop Gore

Men at Work

Work done in the spirit of service is the
highest form of worship . . .
'Abdu'l-Bahá[1]

It is incumbent upon each one of you to engage in
some occupation – such as a craft, a trade or the
like. We have exalted your engagement in such work
to the rank of worship of the one true God.
Bahá'u'lláh[2]

In the Bahá'í Cause arts, sciences and all crafts are
(counted as) worship. The man who makes a piece of
notepaper to the best of his ability, conscientiously,
concentrating all his forces on perfecting it, is
giving praise to God. Briefly, all effort and exertion
put forth by man from the fullness of his heart is
worship, if it is prompted by the highest motives and
the will to do service to humanity. This is worship:
to serve mankind and to minister to the needs of the
people. Service is prayer.
'Abdu'l-Bahá[3]

Well done is better than well said.
Benjamin Franklin

If a man does something good, let him do it again
and again. Let him find joy in his good work. Joyful
is the accumulation of good work.
The Dhammapada[4]

O My Servant! The best of men are they that earn a livelihood by their calling and spend upon themselves and upon their kindred for the love of God, the Lord of all worlds.

Bahá'u'lláh[5]

Concerning the means of livelihood, thou shouldst, while placing thy whole trust in God, engage in some occupation. He will assuredly send down upon thee from the heaven of His favour that which is destined for thee. He is in truth the God of might and power.

Bahá'u'lláh[6]

And what is the noble truth of the path of practice leading to the cessation of stress? Just this noble eightfold path: right view, right resolve, right speech, right action, right livelihood, right effort, right mindfulness, right concentration. This is called the noble truth of the path of practice leading to the cessation of stress.

Tittha Sutta

All humanity must obtain a livelihood by sweat of the brow and bodily exertion, at the same time seeking to lift the burden of others, striving to be the source of comfort to souls and facilitating the means of living. This in itself is devotion to God.

'Abdu'l-Bahá[7]

Do not say, I need not work for my living, but cast my hope on God who supports all living creatures. You must work for a livelihood, and look up to God to bless the work of your hands. Jacob, in alluding to the delivery from Laban's house, says, 'God hath seen the labour of my hands.'

Midrash Tanhuma

Every person must have an occupation, a trade or a craft, so that he may carry other people's burdens, and not himself be a burden to others.

'Abdu'l-Bahá [8]

What is balanced livelihood?

Herein, Vyagghapajja, a householder knowing his income and expenses leads a balanced life, neither extravagant nor miserly, knowing that thus his income will stand in excess of his expenses, but not his expenses in excess of his income.

Just as the goldsmith, or an apprentice of his, knows, on holding up a balance, that by so much it has dipped down, by so much it has tilted up; even so a householder, knowing his income and expenses leads a balanced life, neither extravagant nor miserly, knowing that thus his income will stand in excess of his expenses, but not his expenses in excess of his income.

Vyagghapajja Sutta

It hath been revealed and is now repeated that
the true worth of artists and craftsmen should be
appreciated, for they advance the affairs of mankind.
Just as the foundations of religion are made firm
through the Law of God, the means of livelihood
depend upon those who are engaged in arts and
crafts.

Bahá'u'lláh[9]

It is the duty of those who are in charge of the
organization of society to give every individual
the opportunity of acquiring the necessary talent
in some kind of profession, and also the means of
utilizing such a talent, both for its own sake and
for the sake of earning the means of his livelihood.
Every individual, no matter how handicapped
and limited he may be, is under the obligation of
engaging in some work or profession, for work,
especially when performed in the spirit of service,
is according to Bahá'u'lláh a form of worship. It has
not only a utilitarian purpose, but has a value in
itself, because it draws us nearer to God, and enables
us to better grasp His purpose for us in this world. It
is obvious, therefore, that the inheritance of wealth
cannot make anyone immune from daily work.

On behalf of the Universal House of Justice[10]

But if any provide not for his own, and specially for those of his own house, he hath denied the faith and is worse than an infidel.

1 Timothy 5:8

Every Bahá'í has the duty to acquire a trade or profession through which he will earn that wherewith he can support himself and his family; in the choice of such work he can seek those activities which are of benefit to his fellow-men and not merely those which promote his personal interests, still less those whose effects are actually harmful.

On behalf of the Universal House of Justice[11]

> Support for one's parents,
> assistance to one's wife and children,
> consistency in one's work:
> This is the highest protection.
> Generosity, living in rectitude,
> assistance to one's relatives,
> deeds that are blameless:
> This is the highest protection.
>
> *Mangala Sutta*

Though being well-to-do, not to support father and mother who are old and past their youth – this is a cause of one's downfall.

Parabhava Sutta

... the principle [is] that the man has primary
responsibility for the financial support of the family,
and the woman is the chief and primary educator
of the children. This by no means implies that
these functions are inflexibly fixed and cannot
be changed and adjusted to suit particular family
situations, nor does it mean that the place of the
woman is confined to the home. Rather, while
primary responsibility is assigned, it is anticipated
that fathers would play a significant role in the
education of the children and women could also be
breadwinners.

On behalf of the Universal House of Justice[12]

We make a living by what we get;
we make a life by what we give.

W.A. Nance

Regarding thy question about consultation of a
father with his son, or a son with his father, in
matters of trade and commerce, consultation is one
of the fundamental elements of the foundation
of the Law of God. Such consultation is assuredly
acceptable, whether between father and son, or with
others. There is nothing better than this. Man must
consult in all things for this will lead him to the
depths of each problem and enable him to find the
right solution.

'Abdu'l-Bahá[13]

Everyone, whether man or woman, should hand
over to a trusted person a portion of what he or
she earneth through trade, agriculture or other
occupation, for the training and education of
children, to be spent for this purpose with the
knowledge of the Trustees of the House of Justice.

Bahá'u'lláh[14]

Whatever the progress of the machinery may be,
man will have always to toil in order to earn his
living. Effort is an inseparable part of man's life.
It may take different forms with the changing
conditions of the world, but it will be always present
as a necessary element in our earthly existence.
Life is after all a struggle. Progress is attained
through struggle, and without such a struggle life
ceases to have a meaning; it becomes even extinct.
The progress of machinery has not made effort
unnecessary. It has given it a new form, a new outlet.

On behalf of Shoghi Effendi[15]

Life's Stages

Life is the childhood of our immortality.
                                Johann Wolfgang von Goethe

It never makes sense to wait until your life is in
a perfect state of grace to celebrate its joys and
passages. Never hesitate to celebrate.
                                         Robert Fulghum[1]

Once We Played There My Daughter

Once we played there, my daughter,
at the base of that old elm tree.
That summer another tree had fallen
near the trunk, and we had made
the stricken tree a spring for swinging.
We stood on a thick lowly limb,
you in a printed beige cotton,
adorned with red kettles, tea cups, and sweets.

I would spring first to set the limb in motion,
steadying myself on the branch
that lay transverse above me.
With each bend of the knee,
the freshly fallen wood yielded under the weight,
and bounced back again with the promise
of a fresh delight. You, much smaller, did the same.

And there we did spring and swing
on the creaking branch,
and laugh on that summer's day.
Thick motes of sunshine,
spots of shadow danced across our face
as we swung from high to low, from low to high.
We were dizzy with the thrill of it,
the chance that we might fall off.

You were much younger, then, my little one,
and that fallen tree has long since been cleared away.
The old elm is still there,
but now stands bleak and barren,
newly dusted with the first fall of winter snow
nestled on its branches.

It will be a white Christmas.
One branch arches its back,
and stretches its arms to heaven and says:
'It's Christmas. It's Christmas!'

I sometimes think of those days,
misty eyed for the past,
but thankful for the on-marching present,
still ripe with possibilities,
on its way to other tomorrows,
and wonder if you remember that summer's day
when we swung on the fallen branch . . .

J.A. McLean[2]

From the beginning to the end of his life man
passes through certain periods, or stages, each of
which is marked by certain conditions peculiar to
itself. For instance, during the period of childhood
his conditions and requirements are characteristic
of that degree of intelligence and capacity. After
a time he enters the period of youth, in which his
former conditions and needs are superseded by
new requirements applicable to the advance in his
degree. His faculties of observation are broadened
and deepened; his intelligent capacities are trained
and awakened; the limitations and environment
of childhood no longer restrict his energies and
accomplishments. At last he passes out of the period
of youth and enters the stage, or station, of maturity,
which necessitates another transformation and
corresponding advance in his sphere of life activity.
New powers and perceptions clothe him, teaching
and training commensurate with his progression
occupy his mind, special bounties and bestowals
descend in proportion to his increased capacities,
and his former period of youth and its conditions
will no longer satisfy his matured view and vision.

'Abdu'l-Bahá[3]

The Child at the Window

Remember this, when childhood's far away;
The sunlight of a showery first spring day;
You from your house-top window laughing down,
And I, returned with whip cracks from a ride,
On the great lawn below you, playing the clown.
Times blots our gladness out. Let this with
       love abide . . .

The brave March day; and you, not four years old,
Up in your nursery world – all heaven for me.
Remember this – the happiness I hold –
In far off springs I shall not live to see;
The world one map of wastening war unrolled,
And you, unconscious of it, setting my spirit free.

For you must learn, beyond bewildering years,
How little things beloved and held are best.
The windows of the world are blurred with tears,
And troubles come like cloud-banks from the west.
Remember this, some afternoon in spring,
When your own child looks down and makes your
       sad hear sing.

Siegfried Sassoon

Children's children are the crown of old men; and
the glory of children are their fathers.

Proverbs 17:6

More precious than our children
are the children of our children.
Egyptian Proverb

Being Grandparents

For your Grandchildren you have a special love
When you hear them say
Nannie and Grandad come and play
This can surely make your day.

A Grandchild is a scamp
In many kinds of ways
They bring you worms in paper bags
But love on many days.

A little bunch of flowers
Clutched in a tiny hand
A smile, a cuddle, then a kiss
What more could anyone wish,

What did we do without them
You'll often hear us cry
But when they're tucked up in their bed
As each day has gone by
We look at them with love again
And quietly give a sigh.

Betty Ramus[4]

Life would be infinitely happier if we could only
be born at the age of eighty and gradually
approach eighteen.

Mark Twain

The Gardener

All my father's eyes can rest upon
are rock plants in a cold frame, a brown
decaying fence, some grass, too much stone

and previous failures which stretch back
as far as he can sense. With his fork
he rises infrequently to poke

and prod his plants, slender alibis
with which to hide his long reveries
from his wife's intolerable gaze,

far too late to talk or put things right.
Taciturn, grey, rigid, he will wait
for the end of unavailing flight

to come of its own accord. The dour
twilight deserting him, he stoops lower,
watching plants with love too hard to share.

Peter Hulme

Stepping Stones

The years pass on, silently as night
Closes on the fretful day,
And leave their mark of joy or sorrow,
That brands us as their pay.

The yearnings of our hearts form traces,
Gathered throughout the years;
That we may sing a lilting song,
Or grieve with bitter tears.

Elusive hope – Acute despair –
Whatever life's toll brings;
Are treads on crystal stepping stones,
That exalt to higher things.

Myrtle W. Campbell

Those who in their youth did not live in self-harmony, and who did not gain the true treasures of life, are later like long-legged old herons standing by a lake without fish.

Those who in their youth did not live in self-harmony, and who did not gain the true treasures of life, are later like broken bows, ever deploring old things past and gone.

Dhammapada[5]

You say that you cannot see the kingdom of
goodness and truth on earth. Neither have I seen
it; nor is it possible for any one to see it who looks
upon this life as the sum and end of all. On the
earth, that is to say on this earth . . . there is no
truth; all is falsehood and evil; but in the universe,
in the whole universe, truth has its kingdom; and we
who are now children of the earth are none the less
children of the universe. Do not I feel in my soul
that I am actually a member of this vast harmonious
whole? do not I feel that in this countless assembly
of beings, wherein the Divinity, the First Cause – or
however you may term it – is manifested, I make
one link, one step between the lower beings and the
higher? If I see, and clearly see the ladder leading
from plant to man, then why must I suppose that it
breaks off at me? I feel not only that I cannot utterly
perish, since nothing in the universe is annihilated,
but that I always shall be, and always was. I feel that
besides me are spirits that live above me, and that in
this universe there is truth.

Leo Tolstoy

Man is only happy so long as he can think of
himself as a link in a chain, inheriting from
his ancestors and planning to pass on to his
descendants.

Christopher Hollis

Through my parents I have a history. Through
my children I have posterity.

Jonathan Sacks[6]

Do thou not lament on account of the death of thy
father. Trust thou in God. Rely upon the Kingdom
of Abhá. That father of thine hastened to the
world of immortality and took a share from the
realm of the Merciful and with the utmost joy hath
attained to eternal life in the everlasting universe.
Walk thou also in the footsteps of thy father and
be characterized with his attributes and qualities.
Enkindle thou his lamp and fructify his garden, so
that thou mayest become his real son and worthy of
the favours and gift of the Almighty.

'Abdu'l-Bahá[7]

I was not aware of the moment when I first crossed
the threshold of this life. What was the power that
made me open out into this vast mystery like a bud
in the forest at midnight! When in the morning
I looked upon the light I felt in a moment that I
was no stranger in this world, that the inscrutable
without name and form had taken me in its arms in
the form of my own mother. Even so, in death the
same unknown will appear as ever known to me.

Rabindranath Tagore

Unfinished Business

I reach up to the big round knob on the door.
Round it my unfinished fingers do not meet.
Steam smokes out of my mouth in the hallway.
I have never been into this room alone before.

I step in fear across its cold frontier.
Please God, let it not be a sin for me
unsanctioned to enter here!
A precipice of glass and dark red wood,
shining like water in the winter sun,
lures me to explore for treasures.
Around its feet, kneeling, I pry
for a crack,
when suddenly my heart
stops.

Some accidental sesame reveals
a cavern of ominous delights!
They will kill me if I'm caught. I don't care.
My heart has leapt into my head,
is kicking at my ears.
My hands shake like flames. I can hardly see . . .

. . . a huge black slab stained with red marks
like the footprints of animals or birds bleeding!
Stillness settles like snow. The act I contemplate
muffles and numbs conscience, fear, good sense,

as a deep drift anaesthetizes sheep.
My heart resumes ticking in its proper place
just like the clock upon the mantelpiece,
and my hand is as steady as an altar.
Though my world should crack I would not falter.
Both my unfinished hands and arms can barely slide
the massive slab down from its niche.

I cannot tell what creatures have bled
their prints onto its unresponding darkness.
Innocent as Pandora I am too young, too eager, to
      be warned.
Deliberate as Cain I lift the slab's lid.
Undeserving as Dresden of pictures of nightmares
I never knew that slabs contained, I see lines
men waist-deep in mud, misshapen, maimed. I
shall be damned for this peep into hell too early.

One man in particular whose bandaged silence,
blood-stained, leaning as though asleep against
the dirt and blood-dark mud,
so inconsolable, weary, still
(I know he is not sleeping, but it is like sleep)
chills me more than this room.

What forms a pain inside me deeper
than any name and spins me wildly
beyond the door uncaring if I'm caught
or damned or killed . . . ?

My unfinished mind has almost grasped a new
idea for an old word. I cannot
properly remember what happens next now
now as I stand still again in this entrance hall
unprepared uncertain tiny and afraid.

Peter Hulme

Memas

In Panchgani
in the cold front room
of the small cottage
which she didn't own
she lay still
under the white sheet
beneath the crimson and green
of the freshly cut
half-opened rose
with her headscarf tight
against the breeze
from the open window
still in the pale flowered brown dress
she always wore for travelling

there were many guests that night
her granddaughter served tea in her stead
for everyone who came and went
throughout the cold black hours
and everyone sat down for a time

and talked, told stories,
laughed, wept,
about the days in Yazd
(no one knew how long ago
exactly) when her son at five
after his father died travelled
to India with his uncle on a donkey
when she was so hungry
she fell in search of flour
down the cellar
of the house she served in
and when the sharp-eyed
mistress returned
the flour she'd hidden in her scarf
was running down her face with sweat
and the bruises of her fall
were nothing to the bruises
of her beating for the flour

and in the morning
there was the washing of the body
which the women did
the arguments about
how many layers of cloth
should wrap her round
what should be written
on the ring she'd wear
whether the body should be
carried in a blanket

through the streets
so that the coffin could leave
from her son's house not
from her daughter's house
which had no proper bathroom
in which to wash a corpse
though it was where she had most loved
to clean and wash and cook
until the last
because nobody tried to stop her

in the end
the body was lifted
from where she left it
into the coffin
(I never knew till then
how heavy and cold a small old
dead woman could be)
then the coffin was lifted
into the jeep which drove us
to the big house where we prayed and ate

when the sun was directly overhead
and the dust on the road was slow
to settle and all the children
from the school she'd served
had gathered we drove off
at walking crawling pace to the gulestan
where a large crowd from almost everywhere

waited to see this long life end
in a small grave
under a small tree in bloom

and candles were lit
and joss sticks
and blossoms strewn
all round the grave

and her five year old
great grandson from Hereford
who had known her
only for ten days cried
first when they nailed the lid on
don't let them for she can't get out
and cried again
when they lowered her
down into the steep red soil
for fear she could not climb the sides
and cried again
when they heaved the grey slabs on top
please stop them for the weight will be too
much
and sobbed out loud
when the men threw
buckets of wet concrete
into the grave for smoothing down
to stop the monsoon
resurrecting her

for then he knew
she'd never wake again down there
to play with or serve us

Peter Hulme

Sonnet LXXXV

Yours be a life of pleasure, lapp'd in ease,
      Ease by the nobleness of labour won,
      By service to man's thought and fancy done.
Your calling gives you power men's souls to seize
And lift them skyward. Not alone to please
      The sense, should art go forth beneath the
            sun,
      But, by her beauty, that man may be won
To heights on earth from which heaven clear he
            sees.
      Friends, you will nobly do God's bidding
            here;
Your path pleasantness, through which your feet
      May journey onwards still in joy, not fear,
While love and friendship make your hours,
      how sweet!
The radiance of the eternal day to meet,
      And, with white lives, before The
      Throne appear.

W.C. Bennett[8]

Death proffereth unto every confident believer
the cup that is life indeed. It bestoweth joy, and
is the bearer of gladness. It conferreth the gift of
everlasting life.

Bahá'u'lláh[9]

God, A Loving Father

God is the Father of all.
He educates, provides for and loves all; for
they are His servants and His creation.
Surely the Creator loves His creatures.
'Abdu'l-Bahá[1]

Father of all. Master supreme. Power supreme in all
the worlds. Who is like thee? Who is beyond thee?
I bow before thee, I prostrate in adoration; and
I beg thy grace, O glorious Lord. As a father to
his son, as a friend to his friend, as a lover to his
beloved, be gracious unto me, O God.
Bhagavad Gita II[2]

The earth is one native land, one home; and all
mankind are the children of one Father. God has
created them . . .
'Abdu'l-Bahá[3]

God is the Father of all. Mankind are His children.
This globe is one home. Nations are the members of
one family.
Attributed to 'Abdu'l-Bahá[4]

O Thou kind Lord! Thou hast created all humanity
from the same stock. Thou hast decreed that all
shall belong to the same household. In Thy Holy
Presence they are all Thy servants, and all mankind
are sheltered beneath Thy Tabernacle; all have

gathered together at Thy Table of Bounty; all are illumined through the light of Thy Providence.

O God! Thou art kind to all, Thou hast provided for all, dost shelter all, conferrest life upon all. Thou hast endowed each and all with talents and faculties, and all are submerged in the Ocean of Thy Mercy.

O Thou kind Lord! Unite all. Let the religions agree and make the nations one, so that they may see each other as one family and the whole earth as one home. May they all live together in perfect harmony.

O God! Raise aloft the banner of the oneness of mankind.

O God! Establish the Most Great Peace.

Cement Thou, O God, the hearts together.

O Thou kind Father, God! Gladden our hearts through the fragrance of Thy love. Brighten our eyes through the Light of Thy Guidance. Delight our ears with the melody of Thy Word, and shelter us all in the Stronghold of Thy Providence.

Thou art the Mighty and Powerful, Thou art the Forgiving and Thou art the One Who overlooketh the shortcomings of all mankind.

'Abdu'l-Bahá[5]

He that loveth father or mother more than me is not worthy of me: and he that loveth son or daughter more than me is not worthy of me.

Matthew 10:37

The Pulley

When God at first made Man,
Having a glass of blessing standing by –
Let us (said He) pour on him all we can;
Let the world's riches, which dispersèd lie,
　　　Contract into a span.

So strength first made a way,
Then beauty flow'd, then wisdom, honour, pleasure:
When almost all was out, God made a stay,
Perceiving that, alone of all His treasure,
　　　Rest in the bottom lay.

For if I should (said He)
Bestow this jewel also on My creature,
He would adore My gifts instead of Me,
And rest in Nature, not the God of Nature:
　　　So both should losers be.

Yet let him keep the rest,
But keep them with repining restlessness;
Let him be rich and weary, that at least,
If goodness lead him not, yet weariness
　　　May toss him to My breast.

George Herbert

Every day is a messenger of God.
Russian Proverb

Whatever hath befallen you, hath been for the sake
of God. This is the truth, and in this there is no
doubt. You should, therefore, leave all your affairs in
His Hands, place your trust in Him, and rely upon
Him. He will assuredly not forsake you. In this,
likewise, there is no doubt. No father will surrender
his sons to devouring beasts; no shepherd will leave
his flock to ravening wolves. He will most certainly
do his utmost to protect his own.

Bahá'u'lláh[6]

I believe in the deep blue sky and the smiling water;
I can see through the clouds of the sky and am not
afraid of the waves of the sea.

I believe in the loving friendships given by the
flowers and the trees. Outwardly they die but in
the heart they love forever. Little paths through the
woods I love, and the sound of leaves on the ground
or of a nut falling or even of a broken twig.

I believe that the days to come already feel the
wonder of the days that are passed and will permit
the wonder to endure and increase.

I believe in and love my belief in, and my love for,
all these things and most of all, I believe in and love
the Source of my belief and love.

Ancient Chinese Tradition

. . . the Divinity has many attributes: He is loving and merciful but also just. Just as reward and punishment . . . are the pillars upon which society rests, so mercy and justice may be considered as their counterpart in the world to come. Should we disobey God and work against His commands He will view our acts in the light of justice and punish us for it. That punishment may not be in the form of fire, as some believe, but in the form of spiritual deprivation and degradation. This is why we read so often in the prayers statements such as 'God do not deal with us with justice, but rather through thy infinite mercy.' The wrath of God is in the administration of His justice, both in this world and in the world to come. A God that is only loving or only just is not a perfect God. The divinity has to possess both of these aspects as every father ought to express both in his attitude towards his children. If we ponder a while, we will see that our welfare can be insured only when both of these divine attributes are equally emphasized and practised.

On behalf of Shoghi Effendi[7]

Dry those tears, my daughter, and look upon your Father. Your Father is the least of all things in size, just has He is the greatest of all things in excellence; and since He is very small He is within everything, but since He is very great He is outside everything. See, I am here with you, both within and without,

the greatest smallness and the smallest greatness.
Behold, I say, do you not see? I fill Heaven and
earth, I penetrate and contain them.

Marsilio Ficino

God is One and Alone, and there is none
          other beside Him.
God is One and alone, the Maker of all
          His creatures.
God is a Spirit, deep-hidden from the eye of
          man and from all things.
God is the Spirit of spirits, of creation the
          Spirit divine.
God is God from the beginning; before all
          things were, He was God.
Lord of existence is He, Father of all, God eternal.
God is the One everlasting, perpetual, eternal,
          unending.
From endless time hath He been, and shall be
          henceforth and for ever.
God is hidden, and no man His form hath
          perceived nor His likeness.
Unknown of gods and of men, mysterious,
          incomprehensible.
God is Truth, and on truth doth He live;
King of truth divine is He.
God is life; and man liveth through him,
the Primeval Alone.

Ancient Egyptian

I am always content with what happens; for I know
that what God chooses is better than what I choose.

Epictetus

Be thankful to Me, and to thy parents . . .

Qur'án 31:13

Children, spouse and siblings are not yours.
Dear friends, mother and father are not yours.
Gold, silver and money are not yours.
Fine horses and magnificent elephants are of
        no use to you.
Says Nanak, those whom the Guru forgives,
        meet with the Lord.
Everything belongs to those who have the Lord
        as their King.

Sikh Scriptures[8]

The bounty and power of God is without limit for
each and every soul in the world.

'Abdu'l-Bahá[9]

God is the Father of all; there is not a single
exception to that law.

'Abdu'l-Bahá[10]

A Father's Prayers

In the highest prayer, men pray only
for the love of God . . .
Attributed to 'Abdu'l-Bahá[1]

Lauded be Thy name, O Lord my God! Thou seest
me in this day shut up in my prison, and fallen into
the hands of Thine adversaries, and beholdest my
son (The Purest Branch) lying on the dust before Thy
face. He is Thy servant, O my Lord, whom Thou hast
caused to be related to Him Who is the Manifestation
of Thyself and the Day-Spring of Thy Cause.

At his birth he was afflicted through his
separation from Thee, according to what had been
ordained for him through Thine irrevocable decree.
And when he had quaffed the cup of reunion with
Thee, he was cast into prison for having believed
in Thee and in Thy signs. He continued to serve
Thy Beauty until he entered into this Most Great
Prison. Thereupon I offered him up, O my God, as a
sacrifice in Thy path. Thou well knowest what they
who love Thee have endured through this trial that
hath caused the kindreds of the earth to wail, and
beyond them the Concourse on high to lament.

I beseech Thee, O my Lord, by him and by his
exile and his imprisonment, to send down upon such
as loved him what will quiet their hearts and bless their
works. Potent art Thou to do as Thou willest. No God
is there but Thee, the Almighty, the Most Powerful.
Bahá'u'lláh[2]

O Transcendent and Incomparable Lord!

Thou hast bidden us look to Thee as to our Father in heaven; teach me to keep in my heart this chosen Name of Thine, that I may discern the true ideal of fatherhood, and learn what Thou wouldst have an earthly father be. Strengthen me with Thy Spirit that I may deserve the trust, the obedience and the love of my little ones. Make me remember that they will learn the meaning of fatherhood from their earthly father, and forbid, O Lord, that I by my unworthiness should lead Thy children astray in their first thoughts of Thee. Thou art the Everpresent, the All-wise.

George Townshend[3]

From grief and disease, from the perils of water, he
     saves and protects us in numberless ways.
Foes may assail us with pitiless fury, yet all of their
     blows are astray.
His outstretched hand is our sure protection, safe
     from the hordes of sin.
His mercy extends to the child yet unborn; what
     tribute of praise can we bring?

Guru Gobind Singh

I beseech Thee by Thy Lastness which is the same as Thy Firstness, and by Thy Revelation which is identical with Thy Concealment, to grant that they who are dear to Thee, and their children, and their

kindred, may become the revealers of Thy purity
amidst Thy creatures, and the manifestations of Thy
sanctity amongst Thy servants.

  Thou art, verily, powerful to do Thy pleasure.
Thou art, in truth, the Help in Peril, the Self-
Subsisting.

Bahá'u'lláh[4]

O Lord, my God! This is a child that hath sprung
from the loins of one of Thy servants to whom thou
hast granted a distinguished station in the Tablets of
Thine irrevocable decree and in the Books of Thy
behest.

  I beseech Thy by Thy name, whereby everyone
is enabled to attain the object of his desire, to grant
that this child may become a mature soul amongst
Thy servants; cause him to shine forth through the
power of Thy name, enable him to utter Thy praise,
to set his face towards Thee and to draw nigh unto
Thee. Verily, it is Thou Who hast, from everlasting,
been powerful to do as Thou willest and Who wilt,
to eternity, remain potent to do as Thou pleasest.
There is none other God but Thee, the Exalted,
the August, the Subduer, the Mighty, the All-
Compelling.

Bahá'u'lláh[5]

Praise be to Thee, dear Lord, Who grantest to Thy servants bounty upon bounty. Thou bestowest on us the marriage-blessing of children bringing with them a thousand delights; and in this very gift Thou openest to us of Thy grace a new world of service to Thee, a new road to Thy good pleasure and favour.

Help us, in love and gratitude to Thee, so to direct and train these little ones that they may become men and women after Thine own heart, and may take their place as Thy lamps shining brightly in a dark world.

George Townshend[6]

O God, look on us who with ceaseless care keep watch and ward over these children, and suffer not our anxiety for them to become a sign of lack of trust in Thee.

We acknowledge that they are in Thy safe keeping. It is for Thee to appoint unto them their tasks in life, and Thou wilt bestow on them ample strength and means to perform all that Thou requirest.

Help us to pass on to them the divine Message of the Day of God, to give to them the best we have to give, and doing this, to leave their souls to Thee in perfect trust.

George Townshend[7]

O Thou, the Lover, the Creator and the Lord of
these children, help us their parents to guard and
train them not through human love alone, but as
an act of love for Thee, and of obedience to Thy
command.

Grant us selflessness and devotion, that we may
be able in our hearts to hear Thy bidding, and
understand Thy will for these little ones.

Help us to do for them our utmost in Thy name,
and in calm trust to leave the rest to Thee, the All-
wise Who lovest these Thy children better yet – far
better – than any human parent may love his child.

George Townshend[8]

Let Reverence towards Thee, dear Lord, and
kindness towards all that lives be graven deep into
these children's hearts.

Give to us, their parents, wisdom and
steadfastness, that we may unfold to them, little
by little, at the right time and in the right way, the
knowledge of Thy Truth, and by the example of our
lives may amend whatever is amiss in our teaching.

Let them increase day by day in spiritual strength
that they may learn of Thee the mystery of prayer,
and may attain the reward of conscious communion
with Thy Spirit.

George Townshend[9]

O Father in heaven, Who givest to a parents'
intercession a special privilege, hear Thou our prayer
for these children whom Thou hast entrusted to our
care.

Protect them, we beseech Thee, against the evil
that arises in their own hearts, against the contagion
of their parents' frailties and imperfections, against
the power of those whose hearts are turned from
thee.

Help us to pray for our children with concen-
tration and humility of spirit, and by force of prayer
offered in Thy Name to keep back, far from them,
the evil influences that seek their destruction.

George Townshend[10]

Father, the Sun, bless our children, relatives and
visitors. May our trails lie straight through a happy
life; may we live to be old. We are all your children,
and ask these things with good hearts.

White Calf, Sun Dance Prayer[11]

Praise be to Thee, O God, Who hast given to these
children the boon of earthly life, and brought them
thus far upon the road that leads to life eternal!

O Thou of many gifts, vouchsafe these little
ones the mortal boon of health, prosperity and
happiness; and since these blessings soon must pass
away and be no more, admit them to Thy boundless
worlds of love, endow and so train their hearts that

they may be able to receive and hold fast for ever
in joy the knowledge of Thy coming and Thy glory.
Thou art the All-Compassionate, the All-Wise.

George Townshend[12]

'Of such is the Kingdom of Heaven.'

Grant to these little ones, O Lord, that the gifts
and qualities which now are theirs through weakness
they may make their own by strength. Let them
through all the years retain their child-like heart,
continuing humble and receptive as now, full of
wonder, eager to learn. Increase day by day and year
by year their faith that as the children of a Higher
Home than this they may become heirs of Eternity
and earn the blessed fruits of this Divine Age of
Fulfilment. Amen.

George Townshend[13]

Here, O Lord, within the precincts of Thy
protection, Love is king and Faith and Hope are the
lords of thought. But in the world without, Faith
and Hope wander in a wilderness and a stranger sits
upon Love's throne.

Be Thou, O Lord, the strength and shield of
these little ones from their life's beginning to its
very end. Grant that their love and faith and hope
may prevail against every enemy and put to shame
all doubt and disbelief. Give them fortitude and
power that through childhood and manhood, in

prosperity and in adversity, they may continue that
journey toward Thee which here they have begun,
and may to their lives' end bear witness to Thy truth
and remain firm in Thy covenant.

George Townshend[14]

Praise be to Thee, O God, for Thy bounty to the
weak, the young, the humble, and for Thy power
whereby Thou doest whatsoever Thou willest,
unhelped, unhindered, uncomprehended by the
thoughts of men!

Thou puttest down the mighty, and dost exalt
them of low estate.

Thou hidest Thy mystery from the wise and
learned, and revealest it to them who are as babes.

The scholar and philosopher see and perceive
not, read and understand not; the child beholding
Thy beauty steps into Thy kingdom.

O Loving Lord, Who hast never turned away
from a longing heart, nor an appealing cry, we pray
then by Thy Most Great Name to deal with these
little ones – these tender branches of the tree of life
– according to Thy all perfect knowledge and desire.

George Townshend[15]

O Lord, look upon these little ones, children of Thy
covenant born of those whose hearts are turned to
Thee. Keep them from the first unto the last under
Thy protection and suffer them not to follow any

desire save what may become servants of Thy truth, lovers of Thy beauty.

George Townshend[16]

Hear Thou, O God, our prayer for the children of this Age through the world!

Look with pity on those whose parents have not turned their hearts to Thee nor humbled themselves before Thy Manifestation. By Thy boundless mercy and Thy prevailing will, deliver them out of the darkness that surrounds them, and draw them toward Thy light. Create in their souls a hunger and thirst for righteousness, a longing for spiritual truth; and prepare their minds to listen for Thy voice and to welcome Thy glad tidings.

And now, O God, we beg Thee for these our children and for all others born beneath Thy covenant that Thou wilt endow them with power to recognize and to use to the utmost the blessing Thou hast given them. Grant them strength to stand fast by Thy truth, to uphold Thy cause, and in their time to spread far and near the knowledge of Thy glory and dominion.

George Townshend[17]

O Lord! Help this daughter of the kingdom to be exalted in both worlds; cause her to turn away from this mortal world of dust and from those who have set their hearts thereon and enable her

to have communion and close association with the
world of immortality. Give her heavenly power and
strengthen her through the breaths of the Holy
Spirit that she may arise to serve Thee.

Thou art the Mighty One.

'Abdu'l-Bahá[18]

Father of mine, and of my little son who kneels at
my side and lifts his voice to Thee, hear Thou his
prayer and mine. Protect those whom he loves and
prays for. Lead him onward and ever onward in Thy
way till he shall understand that within his weak
and mortal body is hidden the sacred light of Thine
imperishable Presence.

George Townshend[19]

O Lord! Make this youth radiant, and confer Thy
bounty upon this poor creature. Bestow
upon him knowledge, grant him added strength at
the break of every morn and guard him
within the shelter of Thy protection so that he may
be freed from error, may devote himself to
the service of Thy Cause, may guide the wayward,
lead the hapless, free the captives and awaken
the heedless, that all may be blessed with Thy
remembrance and praise. Thou art the Mighty and
the Powerful.

'Abdu'l-Bahá[20]

Whatever hurt we have done to atmosphere, to
       earth, to sky,
To mother or to father,
May Agni of the house free me from this sin;
May he make me blameless
In respect of all the ill we have wrought.

Prapathaka III[21]

Of His Dear Son, Gervase

Dear Lord, receive my son, whose winning love
To me was like the friendship, far above
The course of nature or his tender age;
Whose looks could all my bitter griefs assuage:
Let his pure soul, ordain'd seven years to be
In that frail body which was part of me,
Remain my pledge in Heaven, as sent to show
How to this port at every step I go.

Sir John Beaumont

To My Child

Just for this morning, I am going to smile
       when I see your face
          and laugh when I feel like crying.
Just for this morning, I will let you choose
       what you want to wear,
          and smile and say how perfect it is.

Just for this morning, I am going to step
            over the laundry
            and pick you up and take you
            to the park to play.
Just for this morning, I will leave the dishes
            in the sink,
            and let you teach me how to put
            that puzzle of yours together.

Just for this afternoon, I will unplug the telephone
            and keep the computer off,
            and sit with you in the backyard
            and blow bubbles.
Just for this afternoon, I will not yell once,
            not even a tiny grumble
            when you scream and whine for the ice
            cream truck, and I will buy you one
            if he comes by.

Just for this afternoon, I won't worry about
            what you are going
            to be when you grow up, or second guess
            every decision I have made where you are
            concerned.
Just for this afternoon, I will let you help me
            bake cookies,
            and I won't stand over you trying
            to fix them.

Just for this afternoon, I will take us to McDonald's
        and buy us both a Happy Meal so you can
        have both toys.

Just for this evening, I will hold you in my arms
        and tell you a story about how you were
        born and how much I love you.
Just for this evening, I will let you splash in the tub
        and not get angry.

Just for this evening, I will let you stay up late
        while we sit on the porch and count
        all the stars.
Just for this evening, I will snuggle beside
        you for hours,
        and miss my favourite TV shows.
Just for this evening when I run my finger through
        your hair as you pray,
        I will simply be grateful that God has given
        me the greatest gift ever given.
I will think about the mothers and fathers
        who are searching for their missing children,
the mothers and fathers who are visiting their
        children's graves
        instead of their bedrooms,
and mothers and fathers who are in hospital rooms
        watching their children suffer senselessly and
        screaming inside that they can't handle it
        anymore.

And when I kiss you goodnight I will hold you a
          little tighter,
          a little longer.
It is then that I will thank God for you,
          and ask him for
          nothing, except one more day . . .

George Arlington

O Thou Who hast blessed us with Thy gift of
children, let not the wonder and the happiness of
these days of their infancy ever pass wholly from
our hearts!

  Grant us a strong undying memory of whatever
is most precious in these fleeting days, that in the
aftertime when our little ones are no longer little we
may still keep in our hearts countless images and
echoes of their babyhood, may see again their open
innocent faces, may hear their voices striving to
imitate their elders' speech and recall these tireless
infant feats of growing knowledge and gathering
strength.

  So shall the unworldly beauty of these childhood
days abide with us forever, and not be wholly lost in
the ripe happiness of the later time.

George Townshend[22]

Prayers for Fathers

Praised be Thou, O Lord my God!
I am Thy servant and the son of Thy servant.

Bahá'u'lláh[1]

Praised be Thou, O Lord my God! This is Thy
servant who hath quaffed from the hands of Thy
grace the wine of Thy tender mercy, and tasted
of the savour of Thy love in Thy days. I beseech
Thee, by the embodiments of Thy names whom no
grief can hinder from rejoicing in Thy love or from
gazing on Thy face, and whom all the hosts of the
heedless are powerless to cause to turn aside from
the path of Thy pleasure, to supply him with the
good things Thou dost possess, and to raise him up
to such heights that he will regard the world even as
a shadow that vanisheth swifter than the twinkling
of an eye.

Keep him safe also, O my God, by the power of
Thine immeasurable majesty, from all that Thou
abhorrest. Thou art, verily, his Lord and the Lord of
all worlds.

Bahá'u'lláh[2]

O my God and my Master! I am Thy servant and
the son of Thy servant. I have risen from my couch
at this dawn-tide when the Day-Star of Thy oneness
hath shone forth from the Day-Spring of Thy will,
and hath shed its radiance upon the whole world,
according to what had been ordained in the Books
of Thy Decree.

Praise be unto Thee, O my God, that we have
wakened to the splendours of the light of Thy
knowledge. Send down, then, upon us, O my Lord,
what will enable us to dispense with any one but
Thee, and will rid us of all attachment to aught
except Thyself. Write down, moreover, for me, and
for such as are dear to me, and for my kindred,
man and woman alike, the good of this world and
the world to come. Keep us safe, then, through
Thine unfailing protection, O Thou the Beloved
of the entire creation and the Desire of the whole
universe, from them whom Thou hast made to
be the manifestations of the Evil Whisperer, who
whisper in men's breasts. Potent art Thou to do Thy
pleasure. Thou art, verily, the Almighty, the Help in
Peril, the Self-Subsisting.

Bahá'u'lláh[3]

. . . I beseech God that He may bestow upon thee
a meek and submissive heart and that He may
confirm thee in the service of the divine garden
and assist thee to emulate the actions and deeds
of the godly ones. Also, that He may guide, to the
Kingdom of God, your father, mother and friends,
in order that by these heavenly blessings they may
become fruitful trees and obtain a portion of the
great and glorious gift.

'Abdu'l-Bahá[4]

I ask from God that thou mayest be the cause of
the awakening and mindfulness of thy father and
mother, and that many of thy friends may rend
asunder the veils of superstition and behold the
Light of Truth.

O thou advancer toward the Kingdom!
Endeavour thou day by day to increase thy yearning
and attraction, so that the attitude of supplication
and prayer may be realized more often.

'Abdu'l-Bahá[5]

I beseech Thee, O my God . . . to forgive me,
and my parents, and my kindred, and such of my
brethren as have believed in Thee. Grant that all my
needs be satisfied, through Thy bounty, O Thou
Who art the King of Names. Thou art the most
Bountiful of the bountiful, the Lord of all worlds.

Bahá'u'lláh[6]

O thou who art imploring God!
I was indeed acquainted with the great
misfortunes and afflictions which have befallen
thee, but I hope that through the bounty of thy
Lord, He may ordain unto thee heavenly fragrance
and spirituality, attractive and internal perceptions
and incorporeal susceptibilities; that He may grant
thee strength after weakness, give thee rest after
trouble, bring thee nigh to Him, and make thee a
sign of His love among all His maid-servants, and

forgive thy father, mother, brother and grandfather
their sins.

Verily, He is the Pardoner, the Forgiver.

'Abdu'l-Bahá[7]

O Lord! In this Most Great Dispensation Thou dost
accept the intercession of children in behalf of their
parents. This is one of the special infinite bestowals
of this Dispensation. Therefore, O Thou kind
Lord, accept the request of this Thy servant at the
threshold of Thy singleness and submerge his father
in the ocean of Thy grace, because this son hath
arisen to render Thee service and is exerting effort
at all times in the pathway of Thy love. Verily, Thou
art the Giver, the Forgiver and the Kind!

'Abdu'l-Bahá[8]

Fathers as Examples

When you follow in the path of your father,
you learn to walk like him.
Ghanaian Proverb

It is Our wish and desire that every one of you may
become a source of all goodness unto men, and an
example of uprightness to mankind.
Bahá'u'lláh[1]

. . . parents must so conduct themselves in front of
their children that, both in words and acts, they will
be a noble pattern for the children to follow.
Attributed to 'Abdu'l-Bahá[2]

If you do bad things your children will follow you
and do the same. If you want to raise good children,
be decent yourself.
Chris, Mescalero Apache[3]

What the child sees, the child does.
What the child does, the child is.
Irish Proverb

. . . a young man who has acquired the habit of
telling lies and has the hardihood to deceive his
father will find it all the easier to do this to
everyone else.

Terence[4]

A greedy father has thieves for children.
Serbian Proverb

I have taught thee in the way of wisdom; I have led
thee in right paths. When thou goest, thy steps shall
not be straitened; and when thou runnest, thou
shalt not stumble. Take fast hold of instruction;
let her not go: keep her; for she is thy life . . . My
son, attend to my words; incline thine ear unto my
sayings. Let them not depart from thine eyes; keep
them in the midst of thine heart. For they are life
unto those that find them, and health to all their
flesh. Keep thy heart with all diligence; for out of it
are the issues of life. Put away from thee a froward
mouth, and perverse lips put far from thee. Let thine
eyes look right on, and let thine eyelids look straight
before thee. Ponder the path of thy feet, and let all
thy ways be established.

Proverbs 4:11–26

. . . what we learn about the nature of the world
when we are growing up is determined by the actual
nature of our experience in the microcosm of the
family. It is not so much what our parents say that
determines our world view as it is the unique world
they create for us by their behaviour.

M. Scott Peck[5]

. . . look at Me, follow Me, be as I am . . .
                                    'Abdu'l-Bahá[6]

Bibliography

'Abdu'l-Bahá. *Paris Talks*. London: Bahá'í Publishing Trust, 1967.

—— *The Promulgation of Universal Peace*. Wilmette, IL: Bahá'í Publishing Trust, 1982.

—— *Selections from the Writings of 'Abdu'l-Bahá*. Haifa: Bahá'í World Centre, 1978.

—— *Tablets of Abdul-Baha Abbas*. Chicago: Bahá'í Publishing Society; vol. 1, 1909; vol. 2, 1915; vol. 3, 1916.

Aristotle, *Physics*. Trans. R. P. Hardie and R. K. Gaye. *Scriptures of the World* (CD). Chandigarh, India: Computers International, n.d.

Aspinwall, Alicia. *Short Poems for Short People*. New York: E.P. Dutton & Co. Inc., n.d.

Avesta: Vendidad. Trans. James Darmesteter. *Sacred Books of the East*, American edn., 1898.

Bahá'í Prayers: A Selection. London: Bahá'í Publishing Trust, 1951.

Bahá'í Prayers: A Selection of Prayers revealed by Bahá'u'lláh, the Báb and 'Abdu'l-Bahá. Wilmette, IL: Bahá'í Publishing Trust, 1991.

Bahá'u'lláh. *Gleanings from the Writings of Bahá'u'lláh.*
Wilmette, IL: Bahá'í Publishing Trust, 1983.

—— *The Hidden Words.* Wilmette, IL: Bahá'í Publishing
Trust, 1990.

—— *The Kitáb-i-Aqdas.* Haifa: Bahá'í World Centre, 1992.

—— *Prayers and Meditations.* Wilmette, IL: Bahá'í
Publishing Trust, 1987.

—— *Tablets of Bahá'u'lláh revealed after the Kitáb-i-Aqdas.*
Haifa: Bahá'í World Centre, 1978.

Bennett, W. C. *The Worn Wedding-Ring, and Other Poems.*
London: Chapman and Hall, 1861.

The Bhagavad Gita. Trans. Juan Mascaró.
Harmondsworth: Penguin Books, 1962.

Blomfield, Lady [Sara Louise]. *The Chosen Highway.*
Wilmette, IL: Bahá'í Publishing Trust, 1967.

Brown, Joseph Epes (ed.). *The Sacred Pipe: Black Elk's
Account of the Oglala Sioux.* Oklahoma City: University of
Oklahoma Press, 1953.

Campbell, Dr Ross. *How to Really Love Your Child.*
Wheaton, IL: Victor Books, 1977.

Compilation of Compilations, The. Prepared by the
Universal House of Justice 1963–1990. 2 vols. [Sydney]:
Bahá'í Publications Australia, 1991.

Dhammapada, The. Trans. Juan Mascaró.
Harmondsworth, Middx.: Penguin Books, 1973.

Esslemont, J. E. *Bahá'u'lláh and the New Era.* London:
Bahá'í Publishing Trust, 1974.

Fulghum, Robert. *From Beginning to End: The Rituals of
Our Lives.* New York: Villard Books, 1995.

Gail, Marzieh. *Summon Up Remembrance.* Oxford: George
Ronald, 1987.

Ghai, O.P. *Excellence in Buddhism.* New Delhi: Sterling,
1992.

— *Excellence in Sikhism.* New Delhi: Sterling, 1992.

— *Excellence in Zoroastrianism.* New Delhi: Sterling, 1992.

Holley, Horace. *Divinations of Creation.* New York:
Mitchell Kennerley, 1916.

Holy Bible. King James Version. London: Collins, 1839.

Ives, Howard Colby. *Portals to Freedom*. London: George Ronald, 1967.

The Koran. Trans. J. M. Rodwell. London: Dent (Everyman's Library), 1963.

Life Eternal. Compiled by Mary Rumsey Movius. East Aurora, NY: Roycroft Shops, 1937.

Lights of Guidance: A Bahá'í Reference File. Compiled by Helen Hornby. New Delhi: Bahá'í Publishing Trust, 5th edn. 1997.

Living Bible, The. London: Tyndale House Publishers, 1971.

Lombardi, Frances G. L. and Gerald Scott Lombardi. *Circle Without End*. Happy Camp, CA: Naturegraph, 1993.

Maḥmúd-i-Zarqání. *Maḥmúd's Diary*. Oxford: George Ronald, 1998.

Marcus Aurelius Antoninus. *The Meditations of Marcus Aurelius Antoninus*. Trans. George Long. *Scriptures of the World* CD.

Maxwell, May. *An Early Pilgrimage*. Oxford: George Ronald, 1953.

McLeod, W.H. (ed. and trans.). *Textual Sources for the Study of Sikhism*. Manchester: University Press, 1984.

Menog-i Khrad ('The Spirit of Wisdom').Trans. E. W. West. *Sacred Books of the East*, vol. 24, Oxford: Oxford University Press, 1880.

O God, My God . . . : Bahá'í Prayers and Tablets for Children and Youth. Wilmette, IL: Bahá'í Publishing Trust, 1984.

Peck, M. Scott. *The Road Less Travelled*. London: Arrow Books, 1978.

Prickett, John (ed.). *Marriage and the Family*. Cambridge: Lutterworth Press, 1985.

Rickerson, Wayne. *Family Fun and Togetherness*. Wheaton, IL: Victor Books, 1979.

Ryan, Marah Ellis. *Indian Love Letters*. Chicago: A. C. McClurg and Co., 1907.

Sacks, Jonathan. *Celebrating Life: Finding Happiness in Unexpected Places*. London: Fount, 2000.

Sacred Books of the East. F. Max Müller (ed.). 50 vols. Oxford: Clarendon Press, 1879–1910.

Sad Dar. Trans. E. W. West. *Sacred Books of the East*, vol. 24, Oxford: Clarendon Press, 1885.

Say It in Verse. An Anthology of Poems by Women of Bedfordshire. Selected and Edited by Nazia Khanum. Bedford: Equality in Diversity, 1997.

Scriptures of the World (CD). Chandigarh, India: Computers International, n.d.

Shoghi Effendi. *The Advent of Divine Justice.* Wilmette, IL: Bahá'í Publishing Trust, 1990.

— *Arohanui: Letters of Shoghi Effendi to New Zealand.* Suva, Fiji: Bahá'í Publishing Trust, 1982.

Star of the West. rpt. Oxford: George Ronald, 1984.

Tao te Ching. Trans. Stephen Mitchell. New York: Harper & Row, 1988.

Terence, 'The Brothers', in *The Brothers and Other Plays.* Harmondsworth, Middx.: Penguin Books, 1965.

Townshend, George. *The Mission of Bahá'u'lláh and Other Literary Pieces.* London: George Ronald, 1965.

Upanishads, The. Trans. Juan Mascaró. Harmondsworth, Middx.: Penguin Books, 1965.

References

Acknowledgements

1. Sacks, *Celebrating Life*, p. 9.

On the Birth of a Child

1. Guru Arjan, *Salok Sahiskriti*, in McLeod, *Textual Sources for the Study of Sikhism*, p. 115.
2. Holley, *Divinations of Creation*.
3. Brihad-Aranyaka Upanishad, 2.4. *Upanishads*, p. 131.
4. Guru Arjan, *Salok Sahiskriti*, in McLeod, *Textual Sources for the Study of Sikhism*, pp. 115–16.
5. Townshend, *Mission of Bahá'u'lláh*, p. 142.
6. Robert Fulghum, *From Beginning to End*, p. 165.
7. From a Tablet attributed to 'Abdu'l-Bahá, in *Bahá'í Prayers* (London).

The Importance of Fathers

1. Letter of the Universal House of Justice, 23 June 1974, in *Compilations*, vol. 1, p. 412.
2. Quoted in Ghai, *Excellence in Zoroastrianism*, 'Duty'.
3. Marcus Aurelius Antoninus, *The Meditations of Marcus Aurelius Antoninus*.
4. 'Abdu'l-Bahá, in *Compilations*, vol. 1, p. 274.

Fathers As Educators

1. 'Abdu'l-Bahá, *Selections*, pp. 127–8.
2. Terence, 'The Brothers', in *The Brothers and Other Plays*, p. 140.

3. 'Abdu'l-Bahá, *Selections*, pp. 126–7.

Educating Fathers
1. Townshend, *Mission of Bahá'u'lláh*, p. 141.
2. Dhammapada, in *Scriptures of the World* CD, D. 17: Impurities.

Fathering
1. Campbell, *How to Really Love Your Child*, p. 131.
2. 'Abdu'l-Bahá, *Tablets*, vol. 2, pp. 262–3.
3. Townshend, *Mission of Bahá'u'lláh*, p. 147.
4. T. Fuller, *Gnomologia*, 1732.
5. Peck, *The Road Less Travelled*, p. 22.
6. Quoted in Sacks, *Celebrating Life*, p. 42.
7. 'Abdu'l-Bahá, in *Compilations*, vol. 1, p. 263.
8. Aristotle, *Physics*, Book 1.

Fathers Educating Children
1. Bahá'u'lláh, *Kitáb-i-Aqdas*, para. 48.
2. ibid. 'Questions and Answers', p. 138.
3. *The Discourses*.
4. Bahá'u'lláh, *Compilations*, vol. 1, pp. 1–2.
5. From a letter of the Universal House of Justice, in *Compilations*, vol. 2, p. 392.
6. Townshend, *Mission of Bahá'u'lláh*, p. 143.
7. *Tao te Ching*, p. ix.
8. Lombardi and Lombardi, *Circle Without End*, p. 16.

9. 'Abdu'l-Bahá, quoted in *Maḥmúd's Diary*, pp. 407–8.
10. 'Abdu'l-Bahá, *Selections*, p. 129.
11. From a letter written on behalf of the Universal House of Justice, 25 July 1984.
12. Gulistan, Admonition 10.
13. 'Abdu'l-Bahá, *Selections*, p. 142.
14. 'Abdu'l-Bahá, in *Compilations*, vol. 1, p. 393.
15. Sad Dar, ch. 51, in *Sacred Books of the East*, vol. 24.

Fathers and Their Families

1. Sacks, *Celebrating Life*, p. 182.
2. From a letter written on behalf of the Universal House of Justice, 1 August 1978, in *Compilations*, vol. 1, p. 412.
3. Wayne Rickerson, *Family Fun and Togetherness*, p. 7.
4. 'Abdu'l-Bahá, *Selections*, p. 279.
5. Sacks, *Celebrating Life*, p. 95.
6. 'Abdu'l-Bahá, *Promulgation*, p. 168.
7. From a letter written on behalf of the Universal House of Justice to all National Spiritual Assemblies, 18 February 1982, revised July 1990, in *Compilations*, vol. 1, p. 414.
8. Sacks, *Celebrating Life*, pp. 100–1.
9. Rickerson, *Family Fun and Togetherness*, p. 16.
10. Lombardi and Lombardi, *Circle Without End*, pp. 40–1.

11. ibid. p. 34.
12. Sacks, *Celebrating Life*, p. 104.
13. 'Abdu'l-Bahá, quoted in *Maḥmúd's Diary*, p. 329.
14. Sacks, *Celebrating Life*, pp. 93–4.
15. *Soma Pavamana*, Hymn XCVII.
16. 'Abdu'l-Bahá, *Promulgation*, p. 144.

Fathers and the Home

1. Bahá'u'lláh, in *Bahá'í Prayers*.
2. 'Abdu'l-Bahá, *Promulgation*, p. 75.
3. Townshend, *Mission of Bahá'u'lláh*, p. 148.
4. ibid. p. 135.
5. From a Tablet attributed to 'Abdu'l-Bahá, in *Bahá'í Prayers* (London).
6. Quoted in Ghai, *Excellence in Sikhism*, 'Home'.
7. 'Abdu'l-Bahá, *Tablets*, vol. 3, pp. 521–2.
8. Prapathaka III, *The Victim for Agni and Soma*, i. 3. 3.
9. 'Abdu'l-Bahá, *Tablets*, vol. 3, pp. 665–6.
10. Hymn LIII.
11. Part 3, Fifth Prapathaka, First Khanda.
12. Avesta, from *Sacred Books of the East*.
13. 'Abdu'l-Bahá, quoted in *Maḥmúd's Diary*, p. 247.

Honour Thy Father

1. Bahá'u'lláh, *Kitáb-i-Aqdas*, 'Questions and Answers', p. 138.
2. 'Abdu'l-Bahá, *Selections*, p. 140.

3. 'Abdu'l-Bahá, *Tablets*, vol. 3, p. 622.
4. 'Abdu'l-Bahá, in *Compilations*, vol. 1, p. 291.
5. 'Abdu'l-Bahá, *Selections*, p. 140.
6. Quoted in Ghai, *Excellence in Buddhism*, 'Family'.
7. 'Abdu'l-Bahá, *Tablets*, vol. 3, p. 180.
8. The Group of Fours, no. 106.
9. Patala 4, Khanda 14.

Fathers' Sacrifices

1. 'Abdu'l-Bahá, quoted in Maxwell, *Early Pilgrimage*, p. 42.
2. ibid. p. 28.

Love

1. Ives, *Portals to Freedom*, p. 45.
2. 'Abdu'l-Bahá, quoted in Maxwell, *Early Pilgrimage*, p. 23.
3. 'Abdu'l-Bahá, *Selections*, p. 27.
4. 'Abdu'l-Bahá, in *Life Eternal*, p. 55.
5. Peck, *Road Less Travelled*, p. 134.
6. 'Abdu'l-Bahá, *Paris Talks*, p. 38.
7. ibid. p. 179.
8. Peck, *Road Less Travelled*, p. 171.
9. Campbell, *How to Really Love Your Child*, p. 54.
10. 'Abdu'l-Bahá, quoted in Maxwell, *Early Pilgrimage*, p. 21.
11. 'Abdu'l-Bahá, quoted in Gail, *Summon Up Remembrance*, p. 238.
12. Campbell, *How to Really Love Your Child*, p. 44.

13. Peck, *Road Less Travelled*, p. 21.

Spiritual Qualities

1. 'Abdu'l-Bahá, quoted in Gail, *Summon Up Remembrance*, pp. 229–30.
2. Bahá'u'lláh, *Gleanings*, p. 262.
3. ibid. p. 305.
4. Bahá'u'lláh, *Hidden Words*, Persian no. 8.
5. Bahá'u'lláh, *Prayers and Meditations*, p. 240.
6. Bahá'u'lláh, *Gleanings*, p. 196.
7. Bahá'u'lláh, *Tablets*, p. 220.
8. 'Abdu'l-Bahá, quoted in Blomfield, *Chosen Highway*, p. 160.
9. 'Abdu'l-Bahá, quoted in ibid. p. 259.
10. Bahá'u'lláh, quoted in Shoghi Effendi, *Advent of Divine Justice*, p. 31.

Fathers: Establishers of Peace

1. Bahá'u'lláh, *Tablets*, p. 84.
2. Bahá'u'lláh, in *Compilations*, vol. 2, p. 328.
3. *Aparigraha Anuvrat*, Five Vows.
4. 'Abdu'l-Bahá, *Selections*, pp. 26–7.
5. Black Elk, *The Sacred Pipe*.
6. Attributed to 'Abdu'l-Bahá, in Ives, *Portals to Freedom*, p. 43.
7. Bahá'u'lláh, *Tablets*, p. 121.
8. Attainment of Peace and Happiness Through Sense Control and Knowledge, 2.64–71.
9. Augustine, *Confessions*, Book 13, ch. 36.

10. Menog-i Khrad ('The Spirit of Wisdom'), *Sacred Books of the East*, vol. 24, ch. 63.
11. 'Abdu'l-Bahá, *Promulgation*, p. 123.
12. 'Abdu'l-Bahá, *Selections*, p. 273.
13. 'Abdu'l-Bahá, *Paris Talks*, p. 29.
14. 'Abdu'l-Bahá, *Promulgation*, p. 163.
15. Bahá'u'lláh, *Tablets*, p. 162.
16. 'Abdu'l-Bahá, *Paris Talks*, p. 57.
17. *Prapathaka* iv, 'The Optional and Occasional Offerings', iii. 4. 10.
18. *Prapathaka* vii, 'The Piling of the Fire Altar', iv. 7. 3.

Men of the New World Order

1. Bahá'u'lláh, *Kitáb-i-Aqdas*, para. 181.
2. 'Abdu'l-Bahá, *Tablets*, p. 10.
3. Rabbi Yisrael Salanter, quoted in Sacks, *Celebrating Life*, p. 183.
4. From a letter written on behalf of the Universal House of Justice to an individual, 25 July 1984, in *Lights of Guidance*, p. 620.
5. 'Abdu'l-Bahá, *Promulgation*, p. 182.
6. 'Abdu'l-Bahá, *Paris Talks*, pp. 183–4.
7. 'Abdu'l-Bahá, *Promulgation*, p. 77.
8. 'Abdu'l-Bahá, *Paris Talks*, p. 133.
9. ibid. p. 163.
10. ibid. p. 169.

Men At Work

1. 'Abdu'l-Bahá, in *Compilations*, vol. 1, p. 313.
2. Bahá'u'lláh, *Kitáb-i-Aqdas*, para. 33.
3. 'Abdu'l-Bahá, *Paris Talks*, pp. 176–7.
4. *Dhammapada*, ch. 9, no. 188, p. 52.
5. Bahá'u'lláh, *Hidden Words*, Persian no. 82.
6. Bahá'u'lláh, *Tablets*, p. 268.
7. 'Abdu'l-Bahá, *Promulgation*, p. 187.
8. 'Abdu'l-Bahá, *Compilations*, vol. 1, p. 3.
9. Bahá'u'lláh, in ibid.
10. On behalf of the Universal House of Justice, in Bahá'u'lláh, *Kitáb-i-Aqdas*, 'Notes', p. 192.
11. From a letter written on behalf of the Universal House of Justice, 19 November 1974, in *Lights of Guidance*, p. 122.
12. From a letter written on behalf of the Universal House of Justice, 9 August 1984, in *Compilations*, vol. 2, p. 386.
13. 'Abdu'l-Bahá, in *Compilations*, vol. 1, p. 98.
14. Bahá'u'lláh, *Tablets*, p. 90.
15. From a letter written on behalf of Shoghi Effendi, 26 December 1935, in *Lights of Guidance*, p. 550.

Life's Stages

1. Fulghum, *From Beginning to End*, p. 181.
2. 'My daughter Mukina was about eight years old at the time I wrote this and will be 30 years old on 10 November 2003.' J. A. McLean

3. 'Abdu'l-Bahá, *Promulgation*, p. 438.
4. Betty Ramus, in *Say It in Verse*, p. 21.
5. *Dhammapada*, ch. 11, nos. 155–6.
6. Sacks, *Celebrating Life*, p. 100.
7. 'Abdu'l-Bahá, *Tablets*, vol. 3, p. 153.
8. Bennett, *The Worn Wedding-Ring, and Other Poems*, p. 183.
9. Bahá'u'lláh, *Gleanings*, p. 345.

God, A Loving Father

1. 'Abdu'l-Bahá, *Promulgation*, p. 267.
2. *The Bhagavad Gita*, pp. 93–4.
3. 'Abdu'l-Bahá, *Promulgation*, p. 468.
4. Attributed to 'Abdu'l-Bahá, in *Star of the West*, vol. 9, p. 98.
5. 'Abdu'l-Bahá, *Promulgation*, p. 100.
6. Bahá'u'lláh, in *Compilations*, vol. 1, p. 171.
7. From a letter written on behalf of Shoghi Effendi, *Arohanui*, pp. 32–3.
9. Raag Gauree, Part 37.
10. 'Abdu'l-Bahá, quoted in Blomfield, *Chosen Highway*, p. 160.
11. 'Abdu'l-Bahá, *Promulgation*, p. 266.

A Father's Prayers

1. Report of 'Abdu'l-Bahá's words as quoted in Esslemont, *Bahá'u'lláh and the New Era*, p. 90.
2. Bahá'u'lláh, *Prayers and Meditations*, pp. 34–5.
3. Townshend, *Mission of Bahá'u'lláh*, p. 141.

4. Bahá'u'lláh, *Prayers and Meditations*, p. 229.
5. Bahá'u'lláh, in *O God, My God . . .* , no. 2.
6. Townshend, *Mission of Bahá'u'lláh*, p. 136.
7. ibid. p. 139.
8. ibid. p. 136.
9. ibid.
10. ibid. p. 137.
11. Lombardi and Lombardi, *Circle Without End*, p. 49.
12. Townshend, *Mission of Bahá'u'lláh*, p. 135.
13. ibid. p. 138.
14. ibid.
15. ibid. p. 139.
16. ibid. p. 140.
17. ibid.
18. 'Abdu'l-Bahá, in *O God, My God . . .* , no. 16.
19. Townshend, *Mission of Bahá'u'lláh*, p. 140.
20. 'Abdu'l-Bahá, in *Bahá'í Prayers*, pp. 38–9.
21. Prapathaka III, 'The Victim for Agni and Soma', i. 8. 5.
22. Townshend, *Mission of Bahá'u'lláh*, p. 137.

Prayers for Fathers

1. Bahá'u'lláh, *Prayers and Meditations*, p. 24.
2. ibid. p. 15.
3. ibid. pp. 232–3.
4. 'Abdu'l-Bahá, *Tablets*, vol. 3, p. 480.
5. ibid. p. 522.
6. Bahá'u'lláh, *Gleanings*, p. 114.
7. 'Abdu'l-Bahá, *Tablets*, vol. 3, p. 114.

8. 'Abdu'l-Bahá, *in Bahá'í Prayers*, p. 65.

Fathers as Examples

1. Bahá'u'lláh, *Gleanings*, p. 315.
2. 'Abdu'l-Bahá, quoted in Gail, *Summon Up Remembrance*, p. 239.
3. Quoted in Lombardi and Lombardi, *Circle Without End*, p. 43.
4. Terence, 'The Brothers', in *The Brothers and Other Plays*, p. 140.
5. Peck, *Road Less Travelled*, p. 203.
6. 'Abdu'l-Bahá, quoted in Maxwell, *An Early Pilgrimage*, p. 42.